*Through touching stories of life with her son, Rita offers huge doses with hope for mommas of super-active children. Practical, comforting words display understanding of all the weary, stressful moments that come with mothering. Beyond encouraging mommas, Rita shows friends how to walk supportively alongside. Her candid stories and specific, creative solutions focus on embracing grace and joy in the midst of hyperactive chaos.*

KELLI JORDAN,
LEADERSHIP DEVELOPMENT MANAGER,
MOPS INTERNATIONAL

*This is a delightful book full of insight and important information to help busy moms and dads parent their "extra energy" child—infant to teen. Parenting is the best and hardest job we will ever have, and Rita's book provides encouragement on the journey.*

CAMERON MEERS,
LICENSED CLINICAL MARRIAGE
AND FAMILY THERAPIST

DAN MEERS,
PROFESSIONAL NFL MASCOT (KANSAS CITY CHIEFS),
MOTIVATIONAL SPEAKER, AND AUTHOR OF WOLVES CAN'T FLY

*Tommy's Wired and Mommy's Tired is an encouraging read for moms struggling to keep up with a high-energy child. Rita is empathic and practical and points the reader back to God whenever possible. I highly recommend!*

JANEL WAGER,
LICENSED CLINICAL PROFESSIONAL COUNSELOR

*Every child is a special gift from God and especially those who come out of the womb with the energy of an F-5 tornado. So you have a hyperactive kid and you are looking for hope? Meet Rita Bergen! Her terrific anecdotes, insights, and biblical truth will aid moms (and perhaps even some dads) from the nursery room to graduation day and beyond.*

ROD HANDLEY,
CHARACTER THAT COUNTS,
FOUNDER AND PRESIDENT

Rita writes as a mom who knows what it's like to be in the trenches of motherhood. She fights hard to remind us all of the greatness of the calling, but with the compassion of one who has stood in our place. I read Rita's book while in a hectic season of caring for my four young children, including a super-active toddler, and I found her book very readable for busy moms. Her words of wisdom came as a call to hope and perseverance, even when my house resembled more of a war zone than a snapshot from a lifestyle magazine.

KIM VANDERHORST,
MOTHER OF FOUR

Every page of Bergen's book is filled with warmth, love, inspiration, experience, and hope. She offers readers an opportunity to see the big picture as moms to extra-active children and to understand they are not alone. **Tommy's Wired and Mommy's Tired** is a wonderful self-help treasure.

B.J. TAYLOR,
WRITER FOR GUIDEPOSTS, CHICKEN SOUP FOR THE SOUL,
AND AUTHOR OF THE MEMOIR **CHARLIE BEAR: WHAT A HEADSTRONG
RESCUE DOG TAUGHT ME ABOUT LIFE, LOVE, AND SECOND CHANCES**

Rita Bergen is the real deal as a follower of Jesus Christ. I think you will enjoy what she has to say.

JOHN HOPLER,
ADMINISTRATIVE DIRECTOR, GREAT COMMISSION CHURCHES

This book is **amazing!** Rita Bergen encourages mothers who are walking the same path that she has already walked. I served as a Chaplain in the United States Army for twenty-four years, and one of my missions was to minister to families whose spouses were deployed to the Middle East. Rita's book would have been so valuable to those mothers who were dealing with the issues that Rita writes about. Mothers will relate to this book because it is written to them by someone who knows what they are going through.

CHAPLAIN (LTC) STEVE QUIGG,
UNITED STATES ARMY

# TOMMY'S WIRED AND MOMMY'S TIRED

Help for Moms of High-Energy Kids
(And Tips for Family and Friends)

## Rita Bergen

ELM HILL

A Division of
HarperCollins Christian Publishing

www.elmhillbooks.com

# Tommy's Wired and Mommy's Tired
## Help for Moms of High-Energy Kids
### (And Tips for Family and Friends)

Published in Nashville, Tennessee, by Elm Hill, an imprint of Thomas Nelson. Elm Hill and Thomas Nelson are registered trademarks of HarperCollins Christian Publishing, Inc.

Elm Hill titles may be purchased in bulk for educational, business, fund-raising, or sales promotional use. For information, please e-mail SpecialMarkets@ ThomasNelson.com.

The stories in this book are for inspiration and encouragement and are not intended as a substitute for professional counseling. All are based on true events. Some names and details have been changed.

Phone numbers and websites listed in this book are provided as resources and do not constitute an endorsement of the beliefs or policies of the represented organizations.

Scripture quotations marked NASB are from New American Standard Bible®. Copyright © 1960, 1962, 1963, 1968, 1971, 1972, 1973, 1975, 1977, 1995 by The Lockman Foundation. Used by permission. (www.Lockman.org)

Scripture quotations marked NLT are from the Holy Bible, New Living Translation. © 1996, 2004, 2007, 2013, 2015 by Tyndale House Foundation. Used by permission of Tyndale House Publishers, Inc., Carol Stream, Illinois 60188. All rights reserved.

**Library of Congress Cataloging-in-Publication Data**

Library of Congress Control Number: 2019920378

ISBN 978-1-400328420 (Paperback)
ISBN 978-1-400328437 (eBook)

FOR MARLA, MY SISTER AND FRIEND:

*Though we lived miles apart, we traveled motherhood together. Thank you for supporting me continually across the miles.*

# Contents

## PART 4. REFLECTING ON THE JOURNEY

# INTRODUCTION

E lectric currents surged and bolted inside my home for years. Such incredible power! By merit of motherhood, I'd acquired the task of managing an over-the-top vivacious child.

Wired!

If you live in the voltage of a super-busy child right now, you know what I'm talking about. Those same electric currents which jolted me are hitting you now. Firsthand. Unquestionably. You've watched friends respond in dismay, shocked. You've probably wondered, "Does anyone really know what it's like to live with this charge 24/7?"

Yes! Others have lived in that surge and understand your life. I mothered a bolt of energy. Now I invite you to jump into my eyewitness account of life with a hyperactive child. Actually, you and I both know that merely reading an account about a storm can't give the same experience as feeling a thunderous shock as lightning splits a tree. Nor can written words emulate the terror you feel when a bolt strikes your roof, igniting a fire and setting your house aflame. Likewise, these pages can barely simulate the actual stress you're going through. Yet a written news report can serve to document the reality of the destructive storm, and a news account will help others understand the suffering endured.

In the same way, *Tommy's Wired and Mommy's Tired* will validate the reality of what you are experiencing and will describe your world to family and friends who watch you stand against that onslaught of bolts.

When a child is *wired*, the mommy is *tired*. Exhausted. The please-can-I-go-to-bed-now kind of fatigue. It doesn't really matter whether your child's high activity level has come from a strong personality or from a neurological issue such as attention deficit hyperactivity disorder (ADHD) or whether the source of all that vigor is a psychological disorder or perhaps a medical disease.[1] Extraordinary motion in a child stresses the mother, resulting in a weary (and often ashamed) mama.

Your active child has slung a bundle of challenges into your world, which has caused you to wonder, "What's a mom to do?" Yes, what can you do? First, it's important to acknowledge the reality and understand that you actually do have a challenge on your hands. So the first section—"Affirming the Realities"—describes and defines the challenges. After that, the second section, "Coping with Feelings," jumps into the emotions you experience, giving insights for survival. The third section delves into various corners of your life through narratives about "Managing Your World." Finally, in "Reflecting on the Journey," we take a peek in the rearview mirror as I reminisce about my Charlie with a view toward giving you hope. ("Charlie? So who is Tommy?" you ask. Stay tuned.) Every section chronicles the world of hyper and gives you tools for enduring.

This narrative will tell you about my years of raising John, Charlie, Joy, and Grace—especially Charlie, my super-active one. Though my purpose is to focus on the mom's side, my stories obviously have to include the problems and challenges my children brought into my world, which means you might wonder if that embarrasses them.

Because of that, I want to let you know I have permission from all my children to tell our stories. (Adult Charlie has even written a letter of encouragement to you at the end. Thanks Charlie!) I also want to assure you that Charlie knows I never considered him to be "my problem child." I always thought of him as a gift to our family. I loved him bunches (and still do), and his presence in our family made us who we were and who we are. And though my children are in the stories, these tales are not really about my children. The stories are intended to be about *me* and how any mother can face the trials brought on by a wired child.

Also, because my children now have professional lives using their given names, we've chosen to use their middle names in these stories. We want to preserve their professional names for Internet search engines. We didn't want *Tommy's Wired...* to pop up if Charlie's given name were googled in a scientific search.

As a gift to you, I've purposely made most chapters short—brief hugs, hope, and help from one mom to another—because when I mothered an active child, I had little time for *anything* and reading was done in snippets. Read a bit at a time, anytime, anywhere. Keep it open. Take it with you. Place it in the bathroom for thirty seconds of reading.

In the pages ahead, you'll notice there's no mention of medications, such as Ritalin. Medical decisions aren't explained nor any professional consultations or psychiatric evaluations for our son. You won't see details about behavior modification plans nor much about which reinforcements I used. This is intentional. Hundreds of books are available to give you advice in these areas, and our family's decisions were just for us. Every family has to weigh its own situation and weigh the advice of its own counselors and physicians and all the other "experts." My goal isn't to give you advice about managing hyperactivity. My purpose is to care for *you*, the mother, by inspiring some courage, perspective, and hope while you face the very challenging work of raising a super-active child.

On the other hand, maybe you aren't the mom, but rather you know a mom with an extra-active child. The stories on the following pages will give you a window into the world of hyperactivity. Have you ever wondered how to encourage your friend, daughter, sister, or wife who is exhausted and losing hope fast? Read on. Every chapter will illuminate an area of life where a mom might be struggling or needing some help. And hang on because the end of the book provides a section of FAQs written especially for family and friends.

By the way, are you now a bit curious about the end of our story—a bit curious about adult Charlie and what he's up to these days? Well, currently Charlie is a sane adult with a PhD, doing research in biology. (He'd say, "Sane? More or less!") He's a lot of fun, and he is—and always has been—a terrific guy.

So back to Tommy. I know you're asking, "If Rita is the mama of John, Charlie, Joy, and Grace, then who is Tommy?" So glad you asked. Get ready to meet Tommy now—or maybe you already know him... or her.

Welcome to the world of wired. Welcome to the power of a super-active child.

# PART ONE

# AFFIRMING THE REALITIES

Your child twirls and spins, causing your world
to twirl and spin—out of control.
And you ask...
What happened to my life?
Are other children like this?
Can my friends understand?
Why does my child cause so much damage?
Does anyone comprehend how exhausting this is?
Affirming your reality is our first step in
exploring this world called *hyper*.

# One

## MEET TOMMY...

## AND CHARLIE

Two-year-old Tommy burst into my classroom like a thrashing fire hose—powerful, out of control, and constantly on the move. With arms and legs in perpetual motion, Tommy dashed around the room. Jessica screamed when Tommy crashed her puzzle to the floor. Blake needed consoling after Tommy's swift kick. Two teachers definitely were not enough for this powerhouse! I tried distracting wiry little Tommy with a jack-in-the-box, but his eyes darted away in seconds. I tried to hold him and comfort him, but I grasped water. He squirted out of my arms and raced away.

After three hours, I was exhausted yet *amazed*. An empty nester now, I had never met another child that so reminded me of my own boy, Charlie.

Another teacher had registered Tommy, so I'd not met his mother. Now I couldn't wait. I wanted to meet her, empathize with her, and say, "I understand your life." I felt pretty sure I would meet a kind-but-exhausted lady who felt condemned by the world. Maybe a little discouraged. Maybe needing a hug.

At the end of class, she arrived. And I was right. Tommy's mom impressed me as a very sincere, gracious young mother, but she was visibly apprehensive about what I might say about Tommy. As I reported the morning's tempestuous events, I also told her how much I liked her son. He reminded me of my own boy. The anxious lines in her face softened as I related similarities between Charlie and Tommy. She became like a sponge soaking in my words. Someone understood! Someone cared about *her* without trying to give advice on how to change Tommy.

The needs of the *mother* of an active child are rarely addressed. With intent to help, many of your friends—and most books—focus on suggestions on how to manage the child. "Train him to obey," asserts your brother. "Set up a star chart and reward her with a toy," the books advise. So you attempt a zillion ideas, wanting to solve your world. But has all that advice helped your exhaustion? Probably not, because when a child's energy is over the roof, the energy a mother exerts in behavior management is *multiplied*. In the same amount of time that one child might misbehave ten times, a hyperactive child can have thirty infractions or more. If the child's mother is dedicated and deals with all the misbehaviors consistently, she has a nonstop, exhausting job. You don't need more recommendations on how to manage your child (at least not today), but rather some help on how to manage and encourage yourself!

Is your tank on empty? Are you needing a refill? Are you the kind-but-exhausted lady who feels condemned by the world? Maybe a little discouraged? Maybe needing a hug?

If you are the mommy of a child like Tommy, the answer is yes.

Whether boy or girl, Tommy or Tomi, your child's supercharged personality has brought challenges you never dreamed of. *Please stop the world, I want to get off*, you think (and feel a pang of guilt for even thinking the thought). Yet you trudge on, grasping for energy—because your energy has been sucked out by your energetic one. You're left dry. Withering on the vine. Crying in the darkness of your room, hoping nobody sees. Or maybe you wish they *would* see and understand.

Where is comfort? Who can be your cheerleader? Who gives help to a mom without making every piece of advice aimed at changing Tommy into a placid, compliant child? (And that isn't going to happen any time soon, so that kind of advice isn't even very helpful, at least not right now.) So you continue to wither, wishing for something or someone who could help you recharge. But who? What? How?

I know that feeling. I've cried those tears. I've said, *Please stop the world, I want to get off.* And in those dry days, and months, and years, I found a way to drink deeply and recharge. I survived because of help I received, which makes me want to reach out to withering mamas.

And what was key for recharging myself while handling a supercharged kid? H-O-P-E. That is, hope gained from broader perspectives. Hope gleaned from truth-filled values passed along by moms who had gone before me and survived. Hope from books. Hope from someone understanding. Hope like the hope Tommy's mommy received just from having a listening ear.

You, too, can be refilled by drinking deeply from the reservoir of hope. Listen to those voices that express empathetic concern for you without blaming you for every detail of your Tommy's misbehavior. Feel understood, and receive enablement for a long life of being a great mother to a wonderful kid.

A refill of hope also will enable you to give hope to your child. All over the world, rambunctious children exert boundless energy. Yet at the core, each one is a precious child. Whether Tomi or Tommy, all hyperactive children need their moms to believe in them. They need hope. They need someone to believe they are terrific and to lavish love on them in the midst of all the necessary behavior management. So get refreshed and get ready to be the one who can give your Tomi or Tommy that boost—now and for life.

Get ready by absorbing some empathy about your life in the cyclone.

# Two

## LIFE IN THE
## CYCLONE

Shhhhrrrr-iii-eeee-kkkkk!

Pain filled my ears, once again, at the sound of Charlie's scream. Shrieking nonstop, my toddler sprinted from the toy box to the bay window, toppling his brother's stack of red and green blocks along the way. Leaving my dishes at the sink, I ran to intervene before big brother John could retaliate and sock Charlie. As I raced to the rescue, I glanced at a row of bottles in the cupboard. Seeing those vitamins, I lamented, *I don't even have time to take a vitamin.*

Do you find that hard to believe—that I couldn't find time to take a vitamin pill? It's still hard for even me to believe, though it's totally true. And it's even harder to describe.

Have you tried describing your whirlwind called hyper? Do your friends believe you? Do they wonder if you are embellishing? You absolutely *know* you aren't exaggerating, and even though you're aware that your stories seem too far-fetched to be believable, you know they are one hundred percent accurate. Right? Your child's hyperactivity is real and totally impacts your life.

You, the mom, live inside a cyclone. Your Tommy is up before the sunrise can split open your sleep-deprived eyes. Yet the day is already going for this active one, and now you are on duty, like it or not. Though your bathroom still wears dirty towels and scattered undies from the night before, new scatterings are already happening around your home. Teddy bears jump, toy trucks dump, and mega blocks bump. Suddenly preschool Tomi leaps onto the sofa and uses it for a trampoline before somersaulting to the floor. Or preteen Tommy climbs the doorframe, springs a backflip, and then races around the room with fists pumping. And when you say, "Stop, Tommy! Look at me and listen," those words fall on deaf ears.

Yes? Isn't this your life inside the cyclone? Not only at home, but wherever you and your child go, the whirlwind accompanies you. You climb aboard a bus knowing that others can read and relax as they ride, but not you. You have to remain on high alert. As soon as you sit down, Tomi is leaning forward, running her fingers along an imaginary road on the back of the seat ahead. Before you can say, "Sit back and sit still," those fingers land in a lady's curly hair. Embarrassed, you pull Tomi back, but her legs turn into drumsticks on the back of that seat, which is *not* okay, and you wrestle her legs into stopping, but her unabated energy then springs into some new form of muscle motion— tapping her fingers, kneeling backward, hanging over the armrest upside down, and sliding to the floor. Finally you and Tomi disembark. Though you're aware that your child's storm impacted others on the bus, you also know that the storm has passed for them and they'll recover. However, for you the storm clings like water and follows like wind. You long for life to be different. You're trying hard to teach and train this impetuous one, but your child's body remains incessantly on the move.

Sometimes you sense friends thinking, "This is outlandish. Just control Tommy!" But *how* do you control nonstop energy? How can you control a cyclone? Your family thinks you *must* be doing something wrong (or so you imagine). "If only you would discipline this child more, she would be calm." Or discipline her less, or in a different way.

The problem is, no matter what you do, the *energy* never goes away, so your immature, energetic child is always headed for trouble, regardless of your efforts. Because of that, you never have the ability to refute the negative judgments of other people. Since the energy remains, the "problem" always remains (in their opinion), which means they easily conclude they are "right" about what you should be doing differently. And you have no way to disprove these suppositions because *nothing* you do changes your child's energy level. The cyclone still spins.

I lived this life in the cyclone for years. My daily schedule consisted of being busy, busy, and busy. Not only was it hard to find a break for swallowing vitamins, but I remember looking at crumbs in my silverware drawer and thinking, *I don't have a single second to stop and wipe out those crumbs.* Each and every day stretched me to the max.

For example, on a typical day I made plans to do a morning errand, feed lunch to the kids, and put them down for naps. Sounds simple, right? Wrong. Imagine it more like this...

After the morning grocery trip, I unbuckle John and Charlie's car seats, and three-year-old Charlie bounds out of the car to grab rocks from our driveway. He manages to hurl multiple rocks at lightning speed before I can run over and intercept his rock-throwing machine (aka arms and fingers). Redirecting him toward the house, I unbuckle our new baby, Joy, and look up to see Charlie hanging from a low branch of a crab apple tree. Have you ever seen a little boy perform acrobatics among pink blossoms in April? It's actually quite impressive.

Enticing Charlie with a promise of lunch, we traipse to the kitchen and the boys settle in their chairs at the dining table. Keeping my grocery-day-lunch tradition, I open a family-size can of SpaghettiOs and hand each boy a bowl of ringed pasta and a banana. This buys me peace and quiet to unload groceries and start putting them in the cupboards while Joy watches from her infant seat.

Only the peace and quiet are short lived because, unfortunately, Charlie's banana breaks while he peels it, and his ensuing screams would make you think an anvil from the ceiling had dropped on his head. Not a happy camper! I try to convince him that each piece of banana tastes the same as a whole banana, but his fury isn't easily subdued. So I offer him a cookie, which calms his tantrum so I can return to my grocery focus. ("A *bribe*?" you ask. Okay, yeah maybe. But remember, I'm trying to get frozen foods into the freezer before we have ice cream puddles!)

After I get cold things put away, I decide I'll have to unload the pantry staples later because now the baby is fussy and needs to be nursed. So I address that immediate need, but meanwhile the boys begin to giggle and act goofy (amazing how a cookie can change a mood). I look up to find Charlie using a now squeezed and squashed banana as finger paint. Can it be that just moments ago he was throwing a tantrum because of a broken banana? Evidently smashed banana is not in the same league as broken banana because now ten thousand banana pieces are a big thrill. Go figure.

Are you catching the drift? I have grocery bags scattered around the kitchen, a baby now needing a diaper change, lunch dishes waiting for cleanup, plus a boy needing a major banana wash. (And he thinks it's funny. Maybe that's better than a tantrum?)

I'll spare you the details of the rest of a typical day, but it would include stuff like Charlie scrambling up and over the sofa and racing around the living room (multiple times), Charlie cranking out drawings of stick people until a pile of papers flows over the table (hyper-artist), Charlie screaming and impulsively wadding up *all* those papers when one stick boy didn't turn out right (perfectionist), Charlie banging on walls (for no apparent reason), and so on.

*Sigh,* I often thought. *Will the action never end?*

I'm telling the truth. Can you relate? Is that you? If so and you've read this far, I commend you because moms who really need a book like this have a hard time finding time to read it! (BTW, if you're a friend of a mommy of Tommy who doesn't have time to read, could you give her some empathy and encouragement from me? Thanks.)

Yes, our action continued for years. My infant Charlie thrashed while he nursed. Two-year-old Charlie wrecked his brother's games and vaulted into and out of his crib. At three Charlie bounced on over-stuffed chairs and scattered overstuffed teddies. Seven-year-old Charlie wriggled and fidgeted at his home desk, often distracted, mostly oblivious to instructions. At eleven Charlie transformed his sisters' quiet Barbie games into leaping, jumping dolls who wreaked havoc in the dollhouse. Fourteen-year-old Charlie kicked and dribbled his soccer ball in the backyard for hours. The energy never went away.

How can I describe life inside the cyclone? It feels impossible, but when you've lived there, you know. Busy-active, hyperactive, attention deficit, and impulsive—these traits of the cyclone child impact your life directly, forcefully, like a hurricane Harvey that hovers and won't leave town. And even though you love your child, and you know the energy is not his fault, and you don't want him to think he's a problem, your questions still burn, "How can I survive this whirlwind, this cyclone of hyper? How can I survive my emotions? What can I do to manage *my* life? Can anyone understand my world of dealing with this impulsivity, this propensity for damage, and this lack of attentiveness?"

Have I described it? Am I over the top? Moms who've lived in the cyclone reassure me I'm not exaggerating. The action is real!

# *Three*

## THE ACTIVITY
## METER

A ll healthy children are active. That's a given. Yet not all kids have the same degree of activity—some measure at the top. Have you ever watched children and marveled at the differences among their activity levels? My wonder began before Charlie's birth as I observed my pregnant belly rippling like a circus tent in a strong wind. The baby inside was performing acrobatics, and I watched the spectacle. As the audience of this prenatal circus, I loved every minute. *How cute.* I watched the motion, and I marveled that an unborn baby could create such action.

Our firstborn son hadn't given such a show while in utero. But this second child was definitely *active.* I could feel somersaults daily. As I counted kicks and punches, sometimes eight simultaneously, I seriously considered the possibility that my doctor had miscalculated the number of babies inside. Was I carrying twins? Surely no one baby could kick eight places at once. But because ultrasound technology was not commonly available, I had to wait for delivery to reveal the truth.

And then he was born—Charles Bergen. Not twins, but one very active baby, screaming at birth like a screech owl stuck on repeat. "Well, he has reason to scream after the trauma of birth," I reasoned. "He'll settle down."

But he didn't. The active babe before birth became a screaming infant night and day. At our two-week trek to the pediatrician's office, the doctor heard the wails and simply declared, "He's a screamer." The tenants in the apartment above asked if we were pulling out his fingernails. They were joking, of course, but they really did wonder what in the world went on down there. Charlie was not a quiet baby. This acrobatic bundle of energy could not settle down.

Already an "experienced" mom of one other child, I tried all my tricks. I walked him, and I rocked him. I nursed him, and I sang. I worked hard to meet all of his needs, wanting to be sure that his crying didn't come from pain or fear. But while being walked, he squirmed and cried. In the rocking chair, he arched his back and screamed. While nursing, he was more likely to flail his arms than to relax. When he finally slept, in just an hour or two, his cries would pierce our solitude again, and the action would resume. Charlie's prenatal circus had become a postnatal nightmare.

At eight weeks I was ready to despair. Sleep deprived, with no end in sight, I wondered how I could go on. Reality set in as the weeks turned into months and Charlie's activity meter continued to top out. I faced a life I had never expected. Charlie was wired, and Mommy was tired!

Yet in those early days, I found a way to keep my head up by focusing on how special Charlie was. He had energy, but he also had gifts yet to be discovered. He was uniquely created from birth for his own distinct purpose in life. Since I had been given this child and this assignment, I considered myself to be the right mother for him. Even though I was exhausted, I trusted that I'd been specially chosen for this special one. Have you thought about that? You are the one who's been chosen to be the mother of your special child. Your life with Tommy isn't easy, but your role is valuable. Cling to that truth.

Charlie was special—just as precious as my first son. Yet Charlie's activity level was definitely more. At first Charlie's incessant muscle motion was expressed as arms and legs waving like flags in a hurricane, flapping and snapping while he inhaled his milk. Nursing didn't relax him; it provided energy for the flags. I had never known a baby like that. Thankfully, the flags didn't go anywhere. They were in a fixed place, observed not chased. His flailing arms and legs stayed with me, a mommy flagpole. Likewise, in the months ahead, when Charlie went through a drum-and-bugle-corps stage in his high chair, I could just watch the show from my armchair stadium, the dining table. His annoying kicking cadence gave background rhythm to our meals, but I didn't have to chase him because he was contained in his hanging high chair.

But my life of merely observing action collapsed when Charlie began to run (he skipped the walking stage), racing around our house like a high-energy car in a NASCAR race. This new stage brought me out of the stadium and onto the racetrack.

I had two choices. I could try to contain him (not likely) or supervise the race. Never was this truer than at church. Since our little church didn't have an organized nursery, responsibility for him fell to me, and I followed him around the track. (Would-be nursery workers probably sang "Hallelujah," knowing they wouldn't have to take responsibility for the racing Bergen toddler!)

A friend, Cathi, watched Charlie and me at church. I didn't realize it, but she was watching and evaluating. She had seen the flag stage. She had seen the drum-and-bugle stage. And now she saw our NASCAR racing stage.

One day this dear lady came to me and said, "Rita, I'm a nurse, and I've seen hundreds of children in my life. But Charlie is the most active child I've ever seen."

"Really?"

I couldn't believe she'd just said that. She'd just declared Charlie to be the most active child of her whole life.

I could only reply, "Wow."

But inside I screamed, *Thank you... Thank you... Thank you, Cathi!* She had just handed me some validation that I desperately needed. Now I knew beyond a shadow of a doubt that I wasn't just imagining the hardships. Charlie was truly a handful.

Actually, you and I both know that Charlie probably wasn't the most active child that ever lived. Who could ever claim that title? Yet right now I want to offer to you what my friend gave to me—affirmation that you really do have a hyper-busy kid. Take a good look at your child and realize it isn't just your imagination. You actually do have a child who may be the most active child the world has ever seen. Your assessment is valid, so affirm your reality. Believe your observations.

Not all children express the same degree of activity, and you have one approaching the top of the scale. Yet while you acknowledge the fact that you have a super-active child, also pause for a minute and think about energy. In and of itself, energy is not bad. Energy is *needed* for constructive initiatives, and your Tommy might someday use his energy for great ventures. For all you know, your child could be the one who saves the planet. Well, maybe not, but look at your child's energy through new eyes and reframe it. View the energy in light of potential. Energy channeled and directed is wonderful. In fact, many adults wish they had more energy. Having a child who deserves the "Most Active Child" title is not necessarily a bad thing. Embrace that reality—and know there are some in the stadium who understand.

# Four

## Broken Stuff

"*Crash!*" My mind flashed back to that sound of tinkling glass, and I exclaimed, "Hey Charlie!"

My thirteen-year-old son turned to listen. (Wow! I had his attention.)

"Do you remember that time you broke our sunroom window a few years ago? What were you playing?"

"I didn't break that window," he corrected in self-defense. "Joy broke it when she kicked her dress-up shoes across the sunroom."

Oh yes, that rang a bell—a dramatic fling of high heels in a moment of make-believe.

Charlie continued his explanation (staking out truth in his own defense).

"I broke the window in the living room door when I threw a football in the house...."

"And the storm door window on the side of the house when I slammed the door too hard...."

"And the back bedroom window practicing baseball outside...."
"And the other bedroom window kicking a soccer ball...."
*"But I didn't break the sunroom window!"*

Silly me, assuming that Charlie had broken every window that had ever been broken. But can you see why I thought that? He was our most usual source of breakage, and more than a few items had received damage with Charlie in the house. Energy has to be absorbed somewhere, and the items in our house often absorbed Charlie's, which meant his parents absorbed the cost (and pain) from damage control. Ouch. Charlie's mere existence blessed us with windows to replace, toys to repair, pages to tape, clothes to mend, and never-ending messes to clean. And, of course, damage never comes at a convenient time.

Charlie helped repair damages when he was old enough and helped pay costs when he acquired the means. But ultimate responsibility for damages by a minor falls on the parents, so we as parents had to absorb the costs of raising a high-energy kid—costs in both money and time.

If you have a high-energy child, you've probably already dealt with the cost countless times. In all children muscle development takes time (years), so young kids don't have complete control of their movements. Also, young children haven't yet developed good judgment or sound reasoning, which leads to bad choices and results in unintended damage. Then when you combine the high energy of a hyperactive child with that normal lack of muscle control and lack of good judgment, it's a recipe for disaster. And who pays the cost?

You.

It takes money to buy new stuff, money that you may not actually have. And it takes time to repair things or clean up. I feel your pain. For example, another crash that cost me time...

This time, rather than working on his homework, eight-year-old

Charlie had decided to run around our dining table while his sisters colored pictures. Typical of his usual haste and impulsiveness, Charlie didn't control his swinging arms.

"*Crash!*" I was in the kitchen cooking when the sound of falling glass and metal pierced my ears. As I turned and raced to the rescue, I heard Charlie yell.

"Don't worry, Mom! Nothing is unbroken!"

Nothing is *un*-broken? Technically that meant everything was wrecked. Rounding the corner, I found a decorative mirror and multiple trinkets scattered all over the floor. But thankfully, this time nothing was actually broken. Charlie had just misspoken, really meaning to say, "Nothing is broken." Nevertheless, I faced the cost of taking time for picking up scattered trinkets and motivating a young, hyperactive boy to help. And in retrospect, "nothing is unbroken" felt like a good description of life with a high-spirited kid.

Are you living in that world of nothing-is-unbroken? Do you feel you're losing time cleaning your messy child—over and over again? Has your bank account taken a hit? The reality of loss leads to feelings of frustration, for sure. And any kind of loss can result in grief, so don't be surprised when you feel blue over lost time and broken stuff. Sadness might linger even after you've chosen to forgive the immaturity of your little growing human. Grief is also sometimes felt as the emotion of anger, so don't be surprised if you feel angry when stuff gets ruined and budgets are busted. Please don't act out that anger on your child, but instead, turn your madness to sadness. It is okay to mourn your losses.

Before I was a mom, I once saw a friend's six-year-old boy knock over a large mirror propped against a wall, and it promptly shattered (yes, into a thousand pieces). Her son panicked, but my friend quickly said, "That's okay, it was going to burn anyway." This was her way of expressing the truth that nothing lasts forever.[2] Her big-picture mentality produced a steady temper in a crisis situation. She valued the child more than the mirror. Her words served me well as I raised my own children. Staying mindful of eternal values was a big help during times of "broken."

What is truly important? Yes, it's costly to raise a child who scatters and breaks stuff. But your investment in teaching and training that child during a crisis is more valuable than anything lost. Keep the big picture in mind to keep you from breaking the child's spirit (or the child!). A window can be replaced—or taped or boarded. A child's spirit is irreplaceable. Have patience. Show some love. And remember that childish destructiveness does not last forever. As the child grows, next year might actually get better.

Let's support one another, mamas, and give each other some sympathy when our worlds get broken. Here's my sympathy to you!

# *Five*

## IMPULSIVE LEGS

"It's time for family devotions!" bellowed Grandpa Bergen. "It's Sunday morning!" Aunts, uncles, and cousins quickly scrambled to the living room at our shared vacation home.

Our Sunday morning "church service" resembled a talent show, a special tradition during the annual family reunion. Each family prepared a skit or song to encourage (and entertain) the others. Our family presented first—a Prodigal Son skit with five-year-old Charlie acting the part of the Prodigal from Luke 15 in the Bible.

"I want a lot of parties!" Charlie declared to the innkeeper in the far-off country (that would be me).

After this wiry Prodigal had squandered all his (pretend) money in "parties," he went to languish among (cute) little piggies (little Joy and baby Grace) until he was famished and came to his senses, deciding to return home.

The father figure in the story (played by daddy, Mike) greeted the returning Prodigal with a bunch of "rejoices" (tosses into the air). No retribution for this wandering son. His Prodigal was safely home and all was well. Love won.

The Bergen clan clapped. "Great job, Charlie! You could be an actor."

Charlie beamed. Then he sat to wait for the next family's act to begin. As Charlie sat perched on the sofa, he entertained himself by watching the action of his three-year-old cousin. Little James trotted past the sofa and then circled again… and yet again. Charlie's eyes followed the motion until he got bored. Springing from his perch to a nearby armchair, he impulsively jumped and danced on the stuffed chair until, of course, his daddy said, "Sit down, Charlie."

Charlie interpreted "sit down" as a cue to keep leaping back and forth from couch to chair. Eventually he compliantly settled on the chair, but his darting eyes still watched his running cousin. All of a sudden…

Boom! Charlie's legs connected with James as he passed and booted the unsuspecting three-year old to the floor. Out of the blue. No warning. Just because there was a moving target to connect with. It wasn't malicious but completely impulsive. James picked himself up, surprised by the suddenness of the hit.

Impulsivity is a common trait of hyperactive children, and this wasn't the first time Charlie had violated the personal space of family and friends. Nor was it the last. Charlie continually engaged in an activity we called "Bothering People." He would trip his siblings without warning. Or he would reach out his hands to grab them as they walked by. Or he would boot cousins just for fun.

I admonished Charlie over and over, "Don't bother people." But just like the impulsive Prodigal in our skit, words alone didn't seem to make much difference. He had to experience life through trial and error, and he only seemed to learn through the repetitive consequences of negative results. So did Charlie ever get it? Yes. But it took a long, long time.

If you have an impulsive Tomi, you've probably been like me and thought, "Why do I have to say this over and over? Why can't she stop and think before acting?"

I get you. The sheer repetition of all your good "commandments" nearly wears a mother out. But don't lose heart. It's good for children to learn the standards of kindness and goodness, especially impulsive children. It will serve them well for life. Your active responses to their impulsive childishness are vital for showing your child the way.

Even though giving reminders and consequences seems endlessly repetitive, these are important for helping your children treat others with consideration and respect. Children need to learn what's expected of them by society, and this will come through your feedback of rewards and correction. Consistency is key. Over time, consistent rewards and consequences can motivate good outward behavior, so keep up the good effort because it's worth it.

Yet in the long run, something even deeper than mere outward compliance is desirable. You want your children to *care* about other people and to be internally motivated to control their hands and feet and mouth without needing a reward from you. True goodness only comes when they inwardly accept and believe the goodness of goodness for themselves.

Ultimately, time-outs and discipline cannot force a child to be considerate and compassionate on the inside. Internalization of goodness will be your child's own process. Your investment in training your child can show him the way, but external discipline only trains external behavior. Each child has her own journey in life, and she will eventually have to make her own decisions about truly caring for others.

Charlie had to decide to own his impulsive legs. I was just a help along the way. He eventually did become a mature, kind adult, and he now refrains from tripping people (thank God!). Yet I can't really boast about his goodness because ultimately it came from his own decisions, not mine.

Actually, Charlie or any of my other children might have made other choices, even with my abundance of lectures, logic, love, and rules. Their inner goodness was for them to choose rather than for me to magically create, but more on that later. Thankfully, my discovery that children have their own journey prevented me from becoming a control freak because I realized that I was not their ultimate "controller." Though I needed to set a brick wall of good standards for them to bump into (a thousand times), I didn't own the child's journey. What a relief.

# Six

## LISTEN UP!

**M**y husband, Mike, wondered if our son might have a hearing problem. I was skeptical since the pediatrician had never mentioned that as a possibility. But I couldn't deny that three-year-old Charlie seemed oblivious to half of what we asked him to do. Giving instructions to Charlie was like asking a cheetah to vote in the next election. He didn't seem to hear or understand a thing as he sped by. Was he becoming deaf?

One day Mike decided to test it out. With Charlie in the living room, randomly playing with (and scattering) toys, Mike snuck into the kitchen and *whispered*, "Charlie, come here and I'll give you some ice cream." Guess who showed up in two seconds. Yep. Charlie got some ice cream, and the hard-of-hearing theory was shot down.

This attention-deficit child wasn't tuned in, definitely. And growing older didn't auto-produce listening ears. His "deaf" saga continued for years and years.

Four-year-old Charlie galloped down the hall on his stick horse, oblivious to the words I'd just spoken. Following him to his imaginary corral, I touched his shoulder and said, "Charlie, look at me."

Charlie turned to look into my eyes. For the next five seconds, I thought I had his attention while I slowly spoke into his gaze, "In five minutes, you'll need to put away your stick horse so we can go get groceries."

In afterthought, I added, "Charlie, can you please repeat what I just said?" Repetition of the info was a way to check whether Charlie had listened. I'd had his eyes, but did I have his ears?

Looking suddenly startled and confused, Charlie exclaimed, "What?"

Charlie had stared at my eyeballs, yet he didn't know *at all* what I'd just said. Charlie hadn't heard or processed a word. Can you believe it? Well, probably the answer is *yes* if your Tommy is tuned in to outer space like Charlie was. And actually, since this same scenario occurred continually, I could believe it, too (which was why I asked the repeat-after-me question).

We needed Charlie to become a listening child who would tune in, trust us, and then obey because the quick movements of hyperactivity meant Charlie could get himself into trouble faster than I could run. If I said, "Stop!" I needed to know he would stop before an oncoming car crushed him. I knew we needed to tackle this issue.

Are you feeling that same pressure? Does your Tommy need to learn to listen? Does obedience seem an impossibility for an attention-deficit Tomi? Listening and obeying are tightly connected, and often a child's safety depends on quickly obeying mom, which means a child needs to listen. Did you know that if you look up the etymology of the word "obey," the root concept means *to listen*? The Latin word for listen is *oboedire* from which we get the English word *obey.*

Charlie's current safety (and future relationships with teachers and bosses) depended on him learning some listening skills. So I crafted a plan of games and rewards to encourage preschooler Charlie to become attentive and respond in obedience—such as the following.

With a paper in my pocket, I tallied every time Charlie carried out my instructions with an "Okay, Mom." When daddy came home, he lifted Charlie in playful tosses, one fling for each and every successful *okay* of the day. "Rejoice!" he would exclaim as he tossed Charlie into the air. Charlie (and John) loved this reward.

We played "Red Light, Green Light" with Charlie's siblings. The fast listener could be a winner!

We pretended "Concert" during lunches. I was the conductor, and at the wave of my hand, Charlie and his siblings could scream or sing or clap. Noise galore! But at my cutoff wave, the noise was to cease instantly. Fun!

We role-played school—to learn "Listen to the Teacher."

We memorized Bible verses. Charlie listened to me read short phrases and then repeated what he'd heard. This required focus, and drops of honey on a finger were the sweet reward for success.

Charlie and his siblings took turns being Simon in "Simon Says."

We played "Stop and Look at Mom When I Call Your Name." Now that was a game with a purpose! It went like this. Charlie could pretend to run away from me. Run, run, run! But as soon as I yelled, "Charlie!" he was to stop and look at my face. If he did it, he got lots of praise (and sometimes a reward, depending on the day). It wasn't a punishment thing—just a game.

Of course, some circumstances did call for negative consequences for refusal to cooperate (a defiant "*No!*"). But for Charlie to make progress in being attentive, games rather than punishment helped a lot.

Teaching Charlie to listen took extra effort on my part. His attention was usually focused elsewhere, not on his mother's voice. I knew the importance of sticking with our plan, but in the short term, it was hard to have hope of him ever learning to listen.

Yet one supplementary thought kept me going. *I have a heavenly Father who wants me to listen to Him.* God had given me, as the parent, a directive to train my child (for everyone's benefit), and I just needed to be faithful to obey his instructions. Because of this principle, I persevered in teaching Charlie to listen up. Teaching my child was my opportunity to obey my Father's wishes, my chance to listen up—*up* to my Father in heaven. So I listened, meaning I obeyed.

Thankfully, eventually Charlie did improve in listening. He even learned to stop quickly and look at me when I called his name. Five years later in a soccer game, as Charlie dribbled the ball past me toward the goal, I yelled "Go, Charlie!" from the sideline. But when he heard the sound of his mother's voice calling his name, he *instantly* stopped dribbling the ball and turned to look at me. He had switched from soccer game to the "Stop and Look at Mom When I Call Your Name" game. Successful listening—but bad timing on my part. I had *ruined* the play. In that moment I instantly learned not to shout Charlie's name at a soccer game because he was too well trained!

Before the birth of my first son, John, I had asked my mother-in-law if she could give any advice for raising children. She had responded, "I don't know, but whatever you do, be consistent!" Never was this truer than in training Charlie's listening. And it's true for you, too. Get a plan, and then be consistent. Don't give up if you don't see the results in a day. And by the way, don't merely copy my plans. Find good, helpful advice for your own situation.

It's easy to get discouraged when a child doesn't listen. Sometimes this leads to the feeling of "I must be a bad mom if I can't get my child to listen or obey." We know others are watching, so having a disobedient child can feel embarrassing. Some of those people even make comments. Ouch.

Though it can feel disheartening to have a child who doesn't seem to hear a thing you say, who is on the back side of the moon outside of radio contact, don't give up. Your careful instruction in fast listening is extremely needed, and your perseverance in training your child is not wasted time. Your side of the equation is the important piece. Your part is to persevere in teaching and training your child. The timing of the outcome will vary for each child, but your diligence over the months and years is valuable. Don't get swayed by the opinions (and impatience) of others.

Have you been fairly diligent and consistent in applying what you know about teaching children? Do you pursue educating yourself on how to raise a hyperactive child? (E.g., advice for training behavior in ADHD kids can be found on the ADDitudemag.com website.[3, 4, 5]) Are you faithful in doing what you know to do? Do you express love and delight to your child? That's success.

And don't forget, you, too, will benefit by learning to listen up—*up* to your Father in heaven.

# Seven

## INJURY PATROL

O h no, yikes! I snatched Charlie just in time as he climbed over his high chair tray with a leg dangling. Whew! That was a close one. At six months my little wiggle worm had mastered the art of high-chair escape. So we got a different high chair, but same story. He was out of the seat belt again in no time. There was no high chair that infant Charlie couldn't conquer, squirming out of *every* seat belt in the twinkle of an eye, with a twinkle in his eye. I could see the headlines now, "Mom on Trial for High Chair Death." Haven't you wondered that, too, dreading that you'll be held accountable for Tommy's self-destruction? I was honestly scared about all the potential mishaps.

Baby Charlie was an enthusiastic, smiling bundle of energy (when he wasn't crying). His twinkling eyes and energetic personality captured our hearts. But his energetic, smiling personality wiggled and giggled its way into all kinds of mischief, so safety was an ongoing issue throughout his childhood. When Charlie began to crawl, no minute was exempt from safety patrol. Just how high or how far can your little one go in four seconds while you grab a tissue? It's unbelievable, isn't it? When Charlie was eleven months, I went out of the room *literally* for a few seconds and came back to find him on top of a table. He'd climbed onto a chair and then onto a table, in microseconds. Whew... again. And he couldn't even walk yet.

Have you felt the pain of people's suspicions as they observe bruises on your Tommy week after week? Do people raise their eyebrows when you try to explain the goose egg on his forehead? Have you cringed when people question the scratches on Tomi's siblings? It's not easy being the mother of a cyclone. Damage is ongoing, and you're held responsible, or so it feels. I feel with you. That's the pain I felt in the ER one day.

I had been holding Charlie's hand at home while I guided him down the hallway toward our living room. Suddenly Charlie resisted forward motion and impulsively fell to the floor while I still grasped his hand. Why he did that I'll never know, but the result is etched in my memory. Charlie screamed and cried, and when he finally calmed, something was wrong with his left arm. He wouldn't use it.

At all.

I tried handing him a favorite teddy bear. Though he obviously wanted to hold his brown fuzzy animal, he could only lift his right arm to grab it. His left arm hung limp. I tried tossing a rubber ball to him, but when he tried to lift both arms for the catch, his left arm just twitched at the shoulder.

Something was definitely wrong, so off we went to the emergency room and discovered yes, it was true. Something was definitely wrong—a dislocated elbow. Evidently Charlie's impulsive fall to the floor had wrenched his elbow as he'd held my hand. You can imagine how I felt as the ER staff explained the dynamics of nursemaid elbow. I stood there dismayed because I'd been the one grasping his hand when he'd had the injury. I could only hope they weren't thinking "child abuser." I desperately hoped they would believe me… that Charlie had suddenly and impulsively fallen to the ground.

Charlie hurt himself innumerable times. When he was seven, he sliced his chin badly tripping up some stairs. He skinned knees on sidewalks and cut himself carelessly at craft time. Thankfully, we only had that one trip to the ER. Yet the combination of impulsivity and hyperactivity created a formula for injury and not only for Charlie but also for anyone in his path. For example, one day toddler Charlie jumped out of my lap so impulsively and energetically that his skull impacted me squarely in the chin… kapow! I almost fainted from that boxer-like hit. After that I *never* allowed my chin to hover over his head. Never ever. Self-protection. That same year Charlie went on a biting spree, and his poor big brother sported teeth marks almost daily. Charlie's impulsive biting was a hard habit to break. As a two-year old, Charlie attacked his baby sister so often and so carelessly that I chose to keep her in a stroller beside me much of the time, just for her protection.

So what's a mother to do? The temptation is to keep your Tommy wrapped in a cocoon. You long to contain him—in your arms, in his room, or by 24/7 screen time. You're tempted to disallow active play. But totally containing a child is neither possible nor healthy. So eventually we mamas have to face the inevitable reality that accidents will happen. And we have to accept that we may get judged as "incompetent"—or worse.

Yet the well-being of the child is the final word, and not just physical well-being, but also psychological well-being. We may get judged for physical bruises, but what will overprotection or ultra-restraint gain for your child? Although your restraint may procure fewer bruises and maybe a few less stitches, overprotection can cause psychological damage to a child. According to Michigan State University Extension, "The greatest drawback of the overprotective parenting style is underprepared children.... According to leadership expert Tim Elmore, when we rescue too quickly and overindulge our children with 'assistance,' we remove the need for them to navigate hardships and solve problems on their own. This prohibits them from becoming competent adults."[6] Other studies have shown that bruises and scrapes actually contribute positively to a child's development.[7]

Knowing this, I had to make a conscious choice to allow my busy Charlie to play freely and take some risks. It was hard to balance safety concerns with freedom, but I knew it was necessary. Did I succeed at avoiding overprotection? Probably not since I'm the fearful type. (Ask Charlie!) But at least I was aware, and I tried. Charlie shinnied up trees, climbed over playground castles, kicked soccer balls, wrestled with his brother, and in the course of childhood, also nursed numerous bruises and blisters.

Safety concerns were a never-ending issue in our house of hyper. Yet sometimes creativity saved the day, like the day I solved the high chair problem for infant Charlie. In a moment of brilliance, I realized there was one type of chair that Charlie couldn't escape, the kind that hangs from a table. His legs had absolutely nothing to push against, so he couldn't climb out. Success!

But only sort of. Now we had to endure his kicking drumbeats to the tabletop while we ate. Sigh. At least he was safe... for now.

# *Eight*

## HYPERACTIVE
## MOUTH

"Mommy, Mommy, look at my worm. I think it's a good fishing worm. Can we put it in the refrigerator until Saturday when we go to the lake?"

"Mommy, come help me! My blocks won't stay stacked. They keep falling over!"

"Mommy, I was looking out the window... and the Smith's dog started barking at a boy on a bicycle... and the boy got mad, so he threw a rock at the dog... and Mr. Smith came out and looked like he was going to go after the boy... but the boy turned around and rode away... and Mr. Smith chained his dog to a tree... and that's why I'm afraid to go to the mailbox to get the mail because the dog might bite me."

Does your super-active child have a super-active mouth? Are your ears tired? Is it impossible to keep up with all the chatter? Babble can be tiring, or annoying, or distracting. It can seem like inconsequential, childish stuff that's not worth the attention. When Tommy's mouth is wired, your ears can get tired.

In my children's younger days, the prattle of little mouths was constant. By default, I easily tuned out nonstop chatter while my mind focused on the task at hand. Listening meant putting my own (urgent) goals on pause.

At some point during those preschool years, Sharon, my pastor's wife, told me about her own commitment. "When my young children want to tell me something, I stop what I'm doing, stoop down, look them in the eye, and listen." *Hmmm, that's great advice*, I thought, so I took her counsel to heart. Going forward, whenever my children came to me with a story or a concern, Sharon's words rang in my ears. Stop. Stoop. Listen.

Have you thought about the treasure you give Tomi when you stop to listen? By carefully listening to seemingly inconsequential stories, you impart significance to your child. Though Tomi may have an extra-active mouth, through chatter she is sharing her heart, and the heart of a child is extremely consequential. Your action of listening communicates, "Tomi, you are so important to me that I will stop what I'm doing and listen to your thoughts." By listening to small talk, you give her the precious gift of being both seen and known. In the end it's not actually small talk but rather "Mommy sees me and knows me" talk.

Also, through active listening, you are cultivating a habit of availability, an availability which will prove crucial when your child needs the comfort which only you can provide. Fear, sadness, loneliness, and anger will surface in Tommy at unexpected times. Are you ready? For example, what do you think I was doing when my boy said, "The dog might bite me"? Probably meal prep or housework—consequential stuff in my own opinion. But my child had expressed fear and needed my ear—right then. Or what about, "Mommy, come help me! My blocks won't stay stacked. They keep falling over!" The need was urgent. Was I paying attention? Moms, we need to practice being ready to stop and listen so we won't miss those opportunities to comfort and validate our children.

Of course, a little triage is needed here. It's probably impossible to listen to every bit of small talk, especially if you have more than one child. You have human limitations in time and availability, and only God can listen to everybody's words all the time. Since you're not God, you'll need to prioritize the urgent things to attend to. As you do, your children learn an important lesson—to believe you still love them even when you listen to another child or attend to something else. As they mature in this kind of trust, they'll gain personal benefit, both now and for a lifetime.

However, when prioritizing the demands on your time, don't forget the main principle. Whenever possible, seek to stop and listen to your child because the saying is true, "The future is now." You are setting a precedent, listening, which Tommy can bank on into teen years and beyond, confident that Mom will listen to me. Paying attention to your children can convince them now and for years to come that they are important to you, important enough to attend both to small talk and deep feelings.

In later years, I was glad I'd followed Sharon's advice. During his teen years, Charlie never stopped coming to me to share his dreams, his fears, his decisions, and even his girl troubles. The early years of listening paid off.

# Nine

## EVERY CHILD
## HAS A GIFT

F our-year-old Charlie approached me with confusion and frustration on his face. He'd been playing with a new Lego set that included the shell of a motorboat. Earlier I had affixed "Police" stickers that made it look like an authentic registered watercraft. Now he asked angrily, "Why did you put the words on backward?"

Baffled, I watched as he compared the word POLICE on each side of the boat, his two little fingers pointing to each corresponding letter, starboard, and port. Suddenly I realized the problem: since he hadn't learned to read yet, he didn't know that words are written from left to right. Thus according to him, POLICE on port side should have read ECILOP on starboard side, a mirror image. In his mind's eye, both of the Ps should have been toward the boat's bow and the Es toward the stern.

Though he had come to me angry, I realized this little guy was using his analytical mind. He'd made an astute observation and then drawn a logical conclusion. *Pretty neat,* I thought, as Charlie puzzled over my explanation and went back to building with his plastic bricks.

I watched Charlie happily play, caught up in the creativity of his imagination. The boat was soon surrounded by a plastic brick marina and a host of other watercraft. A few trucks and airplanes were added, and a small town began to emerge around the imaginary lake.

Seeing Charlie at constructive, creative play gave me a glimpse into the future. I began to see that my busy active boy also had a busy active mind which he wanted to use creatively. Now he built cities, he built space stations, he built with bricks, and he built with cardboard. Occasionally, calm began to settle onto our house, for maybe a couple of hours.

Do you wish you could show me the special talent you see in your super-active child? The unique ability that you see but no one else has noticed? Do you long to share it, but you don't want to boast? Well go ahead. I give you permission to tell it to someone who will share your joy and not think you are bragging. Find that person. Joy is to be shared.

Maybe you haven't seen it yet, but every child has hidden abilities, special gifts. I've known autistic children who became brilliant at history, quiet children who excelled at powers of observation, and mentally handicapped children who possessed the uncanny ability to bring smiles. Please don't worry while you wait for the talents to be unveiled. Time will reveal their special gifts.

Moreover, every *frustrating* trait of a child can be reviewed in a positive frame. Is she strong-willed? She's showing signs of determination, and that's a good thing. Is he bossy? He has latent leadership abilities just waiting to be developed. Is she a pushover? She's showing signs of cooperation, a great characteristic to possess. Every negative has a related positive to hold onto. Look for it, and keep looking until you perceive it.

Yet even before you see the gifts, simply by merit of existence, your active child is special and wonderful. Never forget that. You might think, "But you don't know my child." It doesn't matter. Tommy's value isn't based on what he has done to win your favor, and Tomi's perfect behavior isn't the issue. Like you, all children are intrinsically terrific just because they were born human. Your hyperactive, over-the-top busy child is an amazing treasure.

A vivacious child brings challenges to your life, for sure. You are facing that reality. But in the process, be careful to differentiate between the difficulties (stemming from your child's active behavior) and his personhood (meaning your child's precious inner core). Doing this will enable you to acknowledge your love for your child even while you deal with her frustrating disobedience. Do you get that? You can delight in your child's unique existence and inimitable gifts, even during her high-spirited moments.

Others might not be able to treasure your child like you do. You may be the only one with a vision of what he or she is inside. You may be the only one to recognize the talents. The sweet moments. The dandelion gift. The smile. But you *know*, and you have the special memories.

The week after we'd celebrated Charlie's third birthday, Valentine's Day arrived. In spite of all the challenges, I knew I loved Charlie so much! He was such a precious, valuable little guy, so I wrote him this Valentine, which is still in his baby scrapbook:

Dear Charlie,

I love you and I'm glad God put you in our family. You're our special wiggle worm, but sometimes you change into a cuddle bug and we cuddle up together. Here's a heart that says "I love you!"

Love, Mom.

P.S. You are a terrific boy!

I knew it was true. Charlie was a special little boy, and just like all children, he needed his mommy's love and delight. Delight is crucial for meeting two extremely important needs for children—children need to believe they are loved and they need to know their existence matters. Even a misbehaving child has intrinsic value and needs your love. So look for every opportunity to say, "You are a terrific kid!" because it's true. Be lavish in delight!

# PART TWO

# COPING WITH
# FEELINGS

Tommy's relentless activity has caused
new emotions to burst inside you.
Feelings about Tomi swirl among
all the other emotions in your life.
And you ask...
What do I do with all these feelings?
How can I handle crazy anger?
Why do I feel so embarrassed?
Can laughter ever come back?
Why do I resent advice from my friends?
Coping with feelings is an integral part
of living in your world called *hyper*.

# *Ten*

## MOMMY SHAME

**M**ommy shame. You've felt it. You've suffered it when the day is ruined by your child's hyper-antics. Tommy baffles you. Tomi is frustrating you. You feel out of control. And ashamed.

You've felt it when the childcare worker won't let Tomi return. Ever. Kicked out at age two.

Or the grocery store clerk stares at your child twirling on the floor, wondering what kind of mother you are, condemning you with her eyes.

Or the relatives talk behind your back, and when you catch wind of their words, you hear unsettling opinions. "Be stricter." "Be a better mother." You've cried heart-wrenching sobs from feeling their disapproval, judgment. Shamed.

I know because I've felt it, too. Remember the emergency room with the dislocated elbow? Yep. Shame. And then there was another one of those days...

*Oh wow, one hundred degrees and rising. Unbelievable.* I contemplated the searing heat outside while I relaxed in the vacation cabin my in-laws had rented. *Thank goodness for air-conditioning.* I'd grabbed this chance to rest while Mike's family played dominos in the living room and our boys napped.

A dreaded sound smashed my tranquility. Two-year-old Charlie had awakened from his nap with screaming. I dashed to his bedroom and tried to sooth him, but, like most afternoons, his shrieking continued. When I picked him up, he arched his back and wailed.

I was accustomed to dealing with tantrums after naps, so today was nothing new. Commonly Charlie's screaming would soon subside, and he'd be ready to play. Only on this day we weren't at home dealing with a tantrum alone. We were in the public presence of relatives, which meant I felt mortified. Here I was with a screaming child, and I couldn't sooth him. It didn't matter that he was now two. He cried on… and on… and on, just as he had as a baby. My father-in-law and mother-in-law and sister-in-law and brothers-in-law were all in the cabin, listening and watching. Ugh. Has your child ever had a tantrum in public? It's so embarrassing.

So what did I do? Well, in my state of embarrassment, I grabbed on to an impossible hope of quickly turning this around. I tried to talk Charlie out of his fit, and then I tried to give him snacks, and then I tried to entertain him, and then I tried ignoring him. But this was not a day for Charlie to calm down quickly, and the fit dragged on.

Meanwhile, the family had already made plans to visit castle ruins at Ha Ha Tonka State Park. By the time we were ready to go, Charlie had calmed once or twice, but the process of buckling Charlie into his car seat reignited his fire. And my shame continued. Why couldn't my child be like other children and wake up happy, rested, and ready to have fun? Why did I have to endure this embarrassing situation? What were my relatives thinking of me? Were they tired of hearing the cries?

Did they wish I had more control? Did they think they probably could have done a better job with this child? I felt so ashamed.

By the time we got to the park, Charlie had settled down a bit. I extracted him from his car seat and carried him to look at the castle ruins while his whimpers subsided. The 100° temperature—and my pregnant belly—needed to be ignored while I soothed this little boy who had his own path in life.

While I carried Charlie, I needed to sooth my own tattered emotions, too. Through self-dialog, I analyzed the events of the past hours and concluded that even if relatives thought badly of me, it was good to stay focused on Charlie's needs. Charlie needed my nurture and protection, and I was confident I had worked hard at consoling him. No need for shame. What should I do with my feelings of embarrassment? Well, I'd have to keep my head on straight and fight the shame battle with the truth that people's opinions don't rule the day. What's best for Charlie must rule.

Staying focused on truth was the best way to win the shame battle.

Shame is a common emotion for a mom with a neurologically different child. When atypical stuff happens in public, a mom's embarrassment can feel unbearable. More than one mom has told me stories of their hyperactive child being kicked out of Sunday school, or of their Tommy staging a royal tantrum in the library, or of Tomi dancing a hyper dance in the store aisle. In all these situations, they felt mortified. Feeling embarrassed is completely common, so if you've felt shame, you are not alone.

While stuff is happening, it's easy to imagine that the whole world wishes your child were more "normal" or "perfect" (whatever that is!). You've probably had those thoughts, and people *might* be wishing that, but most of the time, I discovered that no one was truly judging me.

I later found out that during Charlie's royal tantrum at the cabin, my relatives were *not* thinking anything bad about me. In reality they were full of sympathy, both for me and for Charlie. My shame had actually come from my own self-judgment and imagination.

The best help for me came when I realized my own *beliefs* created the shame. Therefore the place to fight the shame battle was in my own mind. I couldn't change the thinking of the world around me, but I could change my own thinking. I could choose to believe that I didn't need people's approval of my good mothering. I could just be a good mom according to what I knew to do, learning and growing from each new situation (possibly even learning from criticism!) but staying focused on what my child needed.

Consequently, when I faced shame from my children's behavior, I learned to focus on my responsibilities rather than on other people's opinions. There was no way to know whether my imaginations about their opinions were true or not. And even if I discovered they really were judging me (because maybe others outright told me or complained or criticized), I could still focus on my responsibilities. By seeking my child's best interest, I could move forward whether I received approval or not. Like a favorite verse said:

*Now we pray to God that you [my children] do no wrong; not that we ourselves may appear approved, but that you may do what is right, even though we may appear unapproved.*[8]

It wasn't easy, but this focus provided a pathway forward time after time. I determined to seek my child's good whether I was approved or not. That helped and brought hope.

And less shame.

# Eleven

## OVERWHELMED

## BY ADVICE

S peaking of opinions, are you floundering under a dump of advice (and even contradictory views) about your Tommy? It can be crazy. Dozens of competing messages from various friends and relatives can start to do you in. Have you been trying to sort through all the recommendations? Are you trying to navigate friendships which seem to have strings attached, strings implying "agree with my opinions and advice or we can't really be friends"?

Lots of advice might be nice if it would truly help, but often the advice doesn't work, and on the downside, suggestions can seem like a backhanded way to imply *you* are the one with the problem. That message comes across as "You should be able to do something to change this situation." And if you haven't yet, the implication says you're probably to blame. Yet those advisors usually overlook the fact that there's no one answer that works like a charm for *every* child. And often they don't understand the special needs that come with hyperactivity or the special needs of the mother.

For me the challenge of multiple opinions came early. The lineup of advisors started in the first few months of Charlie's life. Like mentioned earlier, Charlie's hyperactivity in babyhood included being Inconsolable with a capital I. Charlie did sleep for short periods, but not because I had succeeded in all my efforts to console him. He just finally slept. Then he would waken in an hour or two, cry some more, nurse some, flail around, and sleep some more.

Of course friends and family were aware of my baby's habits. Out of compassion, they offered solutions:

"Give him a bottle to supplement breastfeeding."
"Lay him in a different position."
"Walk the floor with him."
"Rock him."
"Start solids soon so he'll sleep through the night."
"Let the baby cry. He'll learn to sleep if you don't pick him up."
"Don't let the baby cry. He needs to know he can trust you."

So many opinions.

Often overwhelming.

Yet even when I felt overwhelmed from countless counselors, I still remained hopeful that somebody's trick would work, so for the most part, I sort of appreciated the (abundant!) advice. Maybe the latest suggestion would enable me to get more than two hours of sleep at a time. I tried the bottle trick and the solid food trick and oodles of the other suggestions, and, of course, I listened to the counsel of our pediatrician, but, you guessed it, nothing really worked. Sometimes the ideas even backfired. For example, rocking infuriated Charlie. He would arch his back and scream with a major protest as soon as I merely sat in the rocker. Imagine that—an infant who hated the rocking chair. Charlie was just plain active, and since no one's advice could change his energy tank, I remained stuck in that never-ending cycle of exhaustion.

Until the unimaginable happened...

One night shortly after Charlie's first birthday, I awoke to a strange sensation. I felt rested. I looked at the clock and realized that I had slept *four hours*. Four hours of uninterrupted sleep. It had been months since I'd had that luxury, months of hoping someone's advice would work. And to this day, I *cannot* think of any reason that Charlie started sleeping a little longer at age one except that he grew up.

Had I been doing something wrong that first year? Luckily, this was my second child, and I had some perspective. I knew this child was different than the first child. A crying baby didn't necessarily mean I had done something wrong. It meant he was different, that's all.

The hyperactive child is wired for motion. Since you are the mother, you naturally feel responsible. So first of all, realize it's not your fault. Your Tommy has been gifted with a special ability—to be active, continually. Others have noticed (and perhaps complained). Though they give lots of advice (telling you what to do with this "problem child"), you'll need to remain resolute that a child's capacity for energy should not be blamed on the mother.

It's good to listen to advice and consider everything respectfully, but don't put yourself on a guilt trip (that pesky shame factor again). Your baby is unique. Others don't know your child like you do. So pay attention to friends and family, but only act on what you think is best for your child.

Here's the hope I offer on this subject of abundant advice: "Don't get your hopes up!" When family and friends give advice, it might work, but then again it might not. Take it for what it's worth. Try it. But if it doesn't work, realize that it's not the end of the world. Your child will keep growing, and there's always tomorrow.

# Twelve

## SANITY

"**H**elp!" I pleaded with Debbie. "Can you please come talk to me so I can keep my sanity?"

Amazingly, within hours this mother of five arrived to offer some empathy—alone. (Many thanks to her husband!) In just a short time, she was in my house, listening as I unloaded my complaints on her mommy ears. I proceeded to read my list of Charlie's two-year-old faults. (Yes, I had an actual list, which later I saved in his baby scrapbook because, believe it or not, it became a priceless memory.)

"Charlie goes nonstop! I'm at my wits end! Charlie *continually*:

| | |
|---|---|
| Shouts | Kicks |
| Argues | Bites |
| Fusses | Spits |

Stands on and crunches toys
Climbs all over furniture
Throws stuff

Throws tantrums!

Jumps on me

Messes up games

Makes messes with his food

Bangs on everything

And did I mention tantrums?!"

"Repeat this list 14,000 times a day and you have a picture of life with Charlie. Even though I consistently try to teach him and redirect him, he's nonstop energy. *Aarrggghh!*"

As Debbie heard me vent about the events of that day—and weeks and months—all she did was listen and nod her head. This gracious lady patiently listened and affirmed that dealing with Charlie was hard work. Yes, Charlie was active—super-active. Yes, it was hard, but I would make it. I wouldn't go crazy from his activity. Other mothers faced similar days. And Charlie was precious, more than worth it!

Debbie let me talk, and she offered understanding. Actually, in light of her own challenges, I didn't have much right to complain. She had five children ages ten and under, and one of them was a special needs child with Down's syndrome. Nonetheless, I poured out my frustrations, and she listened to me without condemning me. I knew she understood, which infused hope and some new perspectives.

I loved my child, but I needed someone to offer some empathy. Debbie gave that to me, plus a big helping of affirmation. I began to understand that even though I made plans and pursued daily goals, in reality I only needed to live each minute as it came and just manage the moment. By the time she went home, my courage was renewed.

As I tucked Charlie into bed, I thanked God for my boy. In spite of all the training, correction, and frustrations, Charlie was a valuable child. "Charlie, you are terrific," I said and kissed him goodnight, pulling up his little quilt. Walking toward the door, I glanced back to the sight of my hyper-boy impulsively kicking off covers and bolting upright.

And so I stopped to lovingly instruct my son once again in this new moment that I was managing. Mommy-hood was hard, but my child was precious, and I would make it. It felt good to have some hope.

"Good night, Charlie."

Have you ever gone through a dark time when you felt hopeless? Or feared for your sanity? In a curvy, dark tunnel, it's difficult to see the light at the end. And this is not only true for moms of extra-active children but also for all moms everywhere. Uncooperative children, household responsibilities, broken friendships, financial problems, unreasonable bosses, daycare hassles, health issues, and teen rebellion—the pressures of life can at times feel overwhelming. On the darkest of days, please remember that you are not alone. You may feel completely alone, yet other moms have traveled this tunnel and understand. You are not crazy. The pressure of motherhood is real.

Telling your pressures to someone else can be a big help. Don't try to go it alone; we really do need others who can share the load of our internal struggles. Of course it needs to be someone who won't condemn you—someone who can listen, understand, and give timely advice. Find that friend, that counselor, that person who will allow you to be transparent about the things going on in your head.

Yet sometimes a mom really is alone, without support and without anyone to talk to. If you are in that position and feel hopeless, you can find help by calling a hotline. Several organizations and agencies in our country offer this service. Two numbers that my acquaintances and I have found helpful are 1-800-A-FAMILY and 1-800-NEW-LIFE.

These services will listen to your concerns and, if needed, refer you to a professional counselor who can help you. Other agencies can help as well, and your healthcare provider or a pastor can assist you in finding them. Don't stay in the tunnel alone!

# Thirteen

## FEARING THE WORST

*Outbursts of anger...*
*Rebellious backtalk...*
*Fights with other children...*
*Destruction of private property....*

A s I pondered Charlie's track record, my self-talk continued: *These are things that put adults in jail. If Charlie doesn't grow up and change, he'll be in jail.* Not a pretty thought for a mom to have. Yet in reality, I knew adults who hadn't grown up, and they'd experienced serious consequences for life. So sometimes I extrapolated the present into the future and contemplated the worst. Fair to my son? Definitely not. Did I sometimes fear the future? Definitely yes.

One night when Charlie was nearly four, I asked a university student, Laura, to babysit for a few hours. Laura was studying criminal justice, and she was doing a project which would require a phone call sometime during the evening. I told her that was fine.

Since our boys had a *Calvin and Hobbes* record with babysitters, we gave our sons the normal lecture before leaving for the evening: "Listen to Laura or face serious consequences when we return!" They were sobered just thinking of the possibilities.

Laura served supper to the boys and watched them play while she took care of little Joy. Charlie, of course, was his usual boisterous self, goofing off and testing the limits. Toward the end of the evening, Laura said to the boys:

"I have to make a phone call now."

"Who to?"

"A policeman."

"Why?"

"Because we need to put somebody in jail."

"*Us?*" exclaimed a wide-eyed Charlie.

He seriously wondered it. And honestly, at times so did I.

Over time I learned to keep in mind that though my young Charlie was immature (for sure!), he was *not* a criminal. Staying focused on this reality helped give Charlie both hope and confidence. Positive beliefs about a child actually work toward inspiring that maturity. And by remembering that my youngster was merely undeveloped, not a felon, I gave hope to myself, too.

Fears arise because you cannot know a child's outcome while he is still in the formative years. This is scary and can become a heavy burden. Since our culture tends to blame parents for everything, it's extremely tempting to put the burden of the child's outcome onto yourself. But don't do it. True, your child might *appear* to be on the road to disaster, but please don't take on a weighty load of fear.

Yes, you do have a responsibility to respect and love your children. Yes, you pour yourself into training them and teaching them the rules.

You are responsible to them, but not *for* them. In other words, parents are responsible to teach, to train, and to love their children, but in the end, the children are responsible for their own choices. Please don't put the burden of their future choices onto yourself.

I have friends whose children eventually did spend time in jail. I know these ladies; they were, and are, dedicated moms. Yet their children made some poor choices during teen and young adult years, and they bore society's consequences. These moms grieve more deeply than I can begin to understand, and I've cried over the sadness they've suffered and the blame they've faced. I wish I could change our culture of blame. I long to say to grieving moms everywhere, "We don't blame you!"

Do tears flood your pillow night after night from overwhelming feelings of "I've failed as a mom?" Please stop to listen to a gentle question from heaven, God asking you, "Do you think I'm a failure, too?" God, the perfect parent, still has trouble with his children on earth. So even if you could be the most perfect mother in the world, as perfect as God, you can never guarantee the outcome of your child. Rest in the reality that you've done what you can to give your child good things, and accept the fact you can't make Tommy's choices for him. Don't heap blame on yourself.

# *Fourteen*

## SHAKEN

S nip...
I hid my tears while the children watched me cut a single link from the paper chain strung across the dining room, wall to wall. Forty-two links had seemed like such a good idea when we'd started this project. Daddy was out of the country on a six-week business trip, so I'd made a plan to remove one link at bedtime each night to help the children know when he would return. Brilliant. Or so I'd thought.

But now with only six days gone, the cruel snip of only one link was merely reminding me of eternally long days looming ahead. After the snip, the chain looked no different, stretching endlessly as did my unwanted challenge. It wasn't easy to care for four children alone.

The next morning, we made a plan. We piled into the van to visit the local library, get some books, and occupy half the day with an outing and the other half with reading. But Charlie was not a reader, so when we returned, he rebuffed my urgings to look at a book and proceeded to run around the house for a while before settling to color a narwhal in his beloved Whale Coloring Book. That worked… for a while. The day dragged on till bedtime and…

Snip. Eternal days stretched on…

The first five days had been buffered by the arrival of my sister, Marla, and her son from Colorado. The children were overjoyed by their cousin's visit, and my sister's presence gave me the boost I needed. We created a long-distance birthday party for the cousins' grandmother in Kansas. Homemade cards, balloons, and games—all documented with photos. A celebration by proxy. Children smiled broadly for the camera while they blew out candles on a cake. Then we readied a package with an identical cake plus all the photos, cards, balloons, and games. We mailed the parcel to Grandma Dee Dee in Kansas, and the cousins treasured the memories they'd made.

But now with my sister and nephew gone, each day dragged until bedtime when it was time for another…

Snip. And the days crawled unendingly…

Is this story starting to seem long and never-ending? So were my days!

The next Monday I needed to find fresh ways to occupy restless children. Our sandbox entertained for a while until time to come inside from the morning's fun to eat peanut butter sandwiches and red (bruised) apples. After lunch the boys returned to backyard play while I read picture books to the girls before naptime.

Charlie and John found ways to occupy themselves in our fenced backyard, digging holes in the garden and shinnying a pine tree. On their return I discovered clumps of pine sap matted in their hair. Tree fun had a definite downside. I rubbed our "famous" mixture of toothpaste and peanut butter into their matted hair (which always worked wonders on pine-sap hair). Suppertime finally arrived and then bath time for little girls with sandy toes and showers for big boys with peanut butter/toothpaste hair. Bedtime came and it was time for another...

Snip.

My chronic digestive troubles didn't help, another unwanted challenge. All winter and spring, I'd struggled to find foods that would settle without triggering abdominal cramping. Potato chips, rice, cheese, and yogurt had become my staples—not exactly a healthy diet but the best I'd found to avoid debilitating pain. Though I'd lost a lot of weight, I could only bear to eat food that might keep me as pain free as possible, resulting in low energy. The days were long...

Snip. And the eternally long days stretched into lonesome nights...

I awoke one lonely night, aware that the familiar cramping had returned with a vengeance, as strong as many of the labor pangs I'd experienced at the birth of my children. I got up to take my medicine and ride out the waves of pain, knowing eventually they would subside. While I waited it out, I grabbed my Bible and opened to where I'd left off the day before, Psalm 75. I randomly read while I endured the pain, and I noticed God's promise in verse three, "When the earth quakes and its people live in turmoil, I am the one who keeps its foundations firm."[9] The discomforts in my life certainly felt like tremors, for sure. But the verse didn't say people of faith never faced problems. The verse *included* quaking. Yet throughout any trembling, my heavenly Father promised to be an undergirding presence, even in these times of loneliness and pain. That felt hopeful. Eventually I relaxed in bed and drifted off...

Ring... ring... ring.... I answered the early morning bedside call.

"Rita, this is Libby. Is Mike okay?"

"What?" I didn't know how to answer Libby. What was she talking about? Is Mike okay?

"There's been an earthquake in the Philippines," Libby quickly continued. "It was above 7 on the Richter scale and some buildings have collapsed, including a hotel."

"Wow, no I didn't know," I replied. My mind began to absorb the reality. A hotel in the Philippines had collapsed. Mike was in a hotel there. No! I didn't want any new trouble. But *immediately* Psalm 75:3 came to my mind. Just hours before, I had read that when the earth quakes and people are in turmoil, the Lord holds us firmly. The earthquake verse of the night before had prepared me for now. As I listened to Libby on the phone, I listened with full confidence that no matter what news arrived about my husband's welfare, God would be my stability. And even if the outcome was not the news I wanted, I could trust that God had been with Mike during the quake, even if it meant being with him while he suffered a hotel collapse.

News trickled in throughout the day, but nothing definitive. Hour after hour, I tried to call the hotel without luck. I waited and tried to carry on with the children, but it was hard. Being alone had already been hard, and now I was faced with the horror of fearing widowhood.

Yet somehow the verse from the night before felt special and personal. It seemed God had personally prepared me for that day's news by giving me such a specific earthquake verse. Therefore, I could trust Him to be with me to the end—whether to the end of this six weeks or to the end of my life.

Thankfully, at last I was able to make connection with Mike—a brief one-minute phone call that assured me he was okay. His hotel had swayed throughout those minutes of tremors, but it hadn't collapsed. Yet even if it had, my confidence had been renewed that God would be with me through any period of difficulty, just as he was now.

Courage. Perspective. Hope.

Soon bedtime came, and...

Snip. My eternally unending days had been buffered by *eternal reality*. Though the days ahead would still be long and difficult, I'd been reminded that the Ever-Present I AM is a personal comfort in my ever-present now.

Are you being shaken as unwanted challenges pile up in your life? Do unpaid bills overflow your desktop? Is the flu season ravishing your household? Are you a single mom, left all alone to deal with crabby children and household chores? Life is not easy.

Acknowledging that God was with me didn't result in physical ease or emotional waltzing. Not at all. I still had all the same troubles and hassles, but remembering God's presence helped me face life without insane desperation. For me, a means of coping with unwanted or unexpected challenges was to remember I actually wasn't alone. "God is a very present help in time of trouble,"[10] so I could trust that God goes with me through every tremor in life. Always.

Each mom who has a hyperactive child faces many unwanted difficulties. Daily. Hourly. Yet I want to acknowledge that if you are a single mom, you face unimaginable challenges in addition to those hyperactivity trials. I know I can't begin to understand all the challenges that go above and beyond coping with an extra-active child. I only know it's incredibly difficult, and you dig deep for courage every day. Since my own experience was not that of being a single mom, I encourage you to find other resources or books to help you. Seek out single moms who've found their way so you can learn from those who've gone before you. Find a support group. Whether it's in your community or online, a support system can be invaluable.

And most of all, I pray that our Ever-Present I AM will give personal comfort to you in your ever-present now.

# Fifteen

## ANGER

You have deep emotions. Well, actually everyone does, but you feel your own the most deeply. Right? Shame, fear, aloneness, and anger can spring up anytime, anywhere, and often without warning. The feelings can threaten to undo you, and meanwhile you still need to manage both your children and all your other responsibilities. Sometimes the emotions spring from dealing with your hyperactive child, but other times they come just from dealing with life. Either way, emotions can deeply impact your interactions with your children. Passions threaten to derail sensibilities, like the day my anger overwhelmed me...

The chill of snowflakes on my down coat couldn't cool the boiling blood under it. With an afternoon deadline to beat, I stood shoveling icy flakes away from my tires while keeping an eye on Charlie and John as they romped in the snow. I trusted little Joy was staying warm in her car seat while I strained in the driveway to release my Ford from a snowy grasp.

Each week my kindergartener, John, participated in a co-op of enrichment classes. Since I taught the music sections, I would drop off my little ones at Jo's, the babysitter, while John and I participated in the co-op. Today was our day to go.

Only today it was snowing. Earlier in the day, the co-op's administrators had debated the possibility of canceling afternoon classes due to the building snowstorm. I had (desperately) hoped for a snow cancelation since I'd spent the morning suffering from my chronic digestive issues, not to mention the nausea of pregnancy that was my current companion. Plus I had the never-ending effort of managing a hyper four-year old and a busy toddler (who wanted to investigate all the no-noes in our house, requiring constant supervision).

I kept shoveling, and my frustrations grew as I ruminated on the fact that *my husband* had even weighed in on the decision when he was consulted by the school administrators. Though he knew my health situation—indigestion and pregnancy—he'd sided with the rest.

"Go for it," he'd told them.

I knew I wasn't sick enough to call in sick, but I had certainly hoped a snow day would be my savior. It wasn't going to happen. So here I stood, shoveling madness.

*Why couldn't those school administrators see the obvious?* Inwardly my anger bubbled up into a tirade as I scooped the snow. *It's still snowing and getting worse. They've put me and everyone in danger. This is no day for holding classes. Crazy!*

"Get into the car! Now!" I called to the boys. "Or we'll be late!" The snow would likely delay our trip across town.

The drive to Jo's confirmed my worst fears. The swish of ice-encrusted wipers informed me the snow wasn't letting up. Slick streets warned I could end up in a spinout. *Not a day for a pregnant woman to be out and about with young kids*, I angrily concluded.

At Jo's apartment, the kids and I shook the snow from our boots at the door. As I took off Joy's pink snowsuit and helped Charlie put his coat away, I heard Jo's landline ring. It was my husband. He asked Jo to let me know that classes had been cancelled. The administrators had decided it was too snowy after all. I could go home.

Do you imagine I was relieved? Wrong. I was furious! I was furious that the administrators—and my husband—had waited so long to admit the obvious. *Why hadn't they put themselves in our place sooner to imagine what we travelers would be facing? Why hadn't they had some compassion toward moms facing the herculean task of driving a carload of kids through a storm? They must have fantasized, "Maybe it won't be all that bad."* I appreciated their good quality of optimism... but really? *And had they even apologized?*

As I drove home, I knew I needed to regroup. I mentally prepared myself to be civil to my husband and kids throughout the evening. Since I'd already learned there's benefit in choosing kindness as a default mode, I purposed to be nice. I knew I could feel emotional but still choose to act rationally toward my family. At the same time, I also knew at some point I would need to sort through my internal rant. The dialogue of my mind was quarreling nonstop with those administrators, and I knew I was in for a bitter fight with myself about my own bitterness. I knew what I must do.

Late that night, after the children had been tucked into bed and my husband had drifted off to sleep, I stole away to my quiet place. I took out a book and my journal, and I began to process what had happened that day—a day of hardships beyond my control, hardships brought on both by nature and by ill-informed decisions. While reading, I stumbled onto a story about some other people who had faced hardships.

The people in the story had found themselves traveling in the middle of a wasteland, lured by someone else's promise of going to a better place to live. But the spot they were in was anything but "better." It was miserable. They missed the comfort foods of home. They hated the hardships of desert tourism. They feared the trip would never end. And they especially despised the leader who had brought them there. They'd even been critical against God about their situation, so critical that they missed being amazed at God's provisions. Their anger about not getting what they wanted prevented them from being grateful for the good.

Ouch. That story was me.

I remembered another time of being frustrated and angry during my year of sleepless nights with my hyperactive infant. The suffering had seemed like an excruciating trip that would never end, and I'd felt pretty angry (or actually not so pretty). I was angry at my baby. Why couldn't he just shut up and let me sleep? This transitioned into anger at the world (sorry Mike) and anger at God. Since God had *created* the need for sleep, why wasn't he giving me the sleep that *he'd* made me to need. Grrrrrrr.

Then, during those sleepless first months, the answer had come. It had arrived from this same story of the travelers' hardships. They had needed food, just like I had needed sleep, and God had known it. But there had been a deeper need for them, so God had used hardships to build priceless character in those travelers. I remembered that my days of sleepless hardship had transformed me and had built character in me which couldn't have been obtained any other way. (Ugh, that's hard to admit, even now.) I needed to learn patience, trust, perseverance, and gratitude—and even kindness—in depths that I couldn't have gone to without the pain. I learned to trust God more deeply—that he could, if needed, provide my necessities in other ways. And I learned to be grateful for each hour of sleep I got instead of counting the hours of sleep missed.

Wasn't that today's lesson, too? Once again I'd faced hardships beyond my control: sickness, children, ice, and people's decisions. Once again I'd faced the resulting anger. And once again the same story had brought me to the place of decision. I could stay in the place of grumbling, or I could move to gratitude, trusting that today's hardships would be used to bring about something deeper, something good. I decided gratitude was a much better place to land. So I softened. And prayed.

The next day (or even the next week or month), it would be okay to discuss my opinions about the decision-making process with those involved and to tell them of the hardships it had produced. But future discussions with my husband and administrators would only be productive if I could stay objective, not vindictive. Staying in a place of bitterness would only hurt me. By choosing gratitude, I chose what was good. For me and for everyone.

Are you angry? You have my sympathy. Like that snowy day, any event beyond my control tended to frustrate me, not to mention the other challenges brought on by having children. At the birth of my first child, I lost some control over my life, and you did, too. Plus after Charlie was born, I discovered a capacity for anger I'd never known existed. It's not easy to handle a hyperactive, attention-deficit, impulsive little human. It would test anyone's patience. Additionally, all children are prone toward questioning and challenging their authorities—which includes you. These realities often cause angry feelings in moms.

Anger and other emotions are real, but believe it or not, emotions can help you. (I say that gingerly. I hope you're not outraged at the thought.) Joy and anger, laughter and tears—it's good to realize that emotions are not your enemies but rather can become your friends. Even anger? Yes, even anger. But how?

Whenever you take the time to process events, your emotions actually alert you to what's going on in your world, such as recognizing an abusive relationship. Your emotions can also teach you about what's happening in your own heart. Pay attention to your emotions to discover what you are believing about others, yourself, and God. Listen to the lessons you learn.

By the way, if you happen to get stuck merely blaming someone else for your anger, or even stuck blaming God, you'll miss a learning opportunity for yourself. So stop and really think about what you are believing about *yourself* in the situation. Then think about what *you* can do to respond in your situation. No matter how much at fault someone else is (and believe me, they can be!), you are still responsible for your own responses. You own that. So take the time to understand your beliefs so you can craft an appropriate response. Analyze your needs and process your pain by taking the time to think things through.

I've found that counselors and friends are a big help in processing my emotions. If possible, find a sensible person who can give you some perspective and help you navigate relational issues. Also, if you've ever been tempted to act out your anger by hurting your child, *get help now*. Internal feelings of anger don't have to result in abusing the child. Just like you control your words and your voice tone around a boss or a guest, you can control your outward actions toward your children. Never act out your frustrations on a child. Rather, admit your problem of anger management to someone you can trust, and get help.

During my parenting years, I also discovered that having a pre-determined plan for responding to my child's misbehavior kept me calmer, less frustrated in the moment. For example, when Charlie had a tendency to hit other kids, I would tell him ahead of time what behavior I expected from him and what the consequences would be if he hit again. As stated by Dr. Carol Brady, "Let your child know the specific consequences she will face the next time she resorts to physical aggression. Depending upon your child's age, the consequences might include a time-out, writing a letter of apology, losing a special privilege, and so on."[11] Without a plan, my anger was prone to rise at each infraction, which tempted me to express myself as a frustrated mama. But with a plan, I could focus my response on the predetermined course of action, which kept me more even tempered.

Lastly, faith can help with anger, too. After my snowstorm tirade, faith helped me find truths to anchor into. Truths about God's bigger picture changed me (even though others hadn't changed yet), and these truths kept my heart from becoming bitter. I didn't want bitterness to define my life, and I'm guessing you don't want that either.

So whenever you feel angry, don't beat yourself up for the feelings inside of you. When anger flares up in you, learn from it as from a friend, admit your pain, analyze it, share it with trusted counselors, and know that millions of moms, like you, are dealing with those feelings of angry grief. We understand that battle!

# Sixteen

## HAPPY MOMENTS,
## GOOD TIMES

L ittle Charlie tugged at my jeans.
"Cum 'ere!" he begged.

He grabbed my finger and led me to a chair.

With teeny, tiny, high-pitched two-year-old babble words, Charlie narrated an unfolding charade in his limited vocabulary.

"Op'n th' gate." Charlie made motions of opening an imaginary gate and walking through it to face me while I sat.

"Thut th' gate." He pretended to turn and shut the gate. Then he walked around in circles in front of me.

"Op'n th' gate." Turning back to the place of the imaginary gate, Charlie "opened" it and exited.

"Thut th' gate" Now he pretended to close that gate and stay outside of it, walking in circles on the other side of the room.

"Op'n th' gate." Charlie reapproached me and came back "in."

"Thut th' gate." Inside the imaginary enclosure, he once again turned to "shut the gate."

Then, surprise... surprise... Charlie scrambled into my lap with open arms. What?

"Hug a cow!" he said.

Ah, sweet moment. With my son in my lap, hugging me, I realized that all along he had been pretending to be a cow going into and out of a fenced pasture!

A cow who loved his mother dearly and wanted her affection.

Precious moments often arrive at unexpected times, but what joy they bring. When joy arrives, make an effort to capture the good and cache it in your memory. Let your little cow hug you, and enjoy the moment while you create a memory. After all, your children won't be with you forever, and you'll especially treasure all your memories when they're grown. So purpose to collect those moments now in the treasure chest of your mind—a collection of gems that will give life-long hugs.

When I was a preschooler, my mother faithfully wrote down the cute sayings of her two children. To make this convenient, she taped a piece of paper inside the door of a kitchen cupboard. Whenever we said something humorous, she grabbed a pencil and wrote it on the paper. Today my sister and I thoroughly enjoy reading these funny quips. There's even one of my older sister saying, "Mother, go write that down!" after I had said something cute.

I decided to follow my mother's example. When my children were little, I kept a piece of paper taped inside a cupboard door, adding new papers as they filled. Today these written anecdotes are priceless to me, and they include the memory of my huggable little cow. Capture your little one's funny sayings by writing them down. Since your children will soon be grown, collecting their cute stories now will capture the memories (and will help you stay focused on their positives in the present).

Speaking of the limited time of child-raising, one warning is in order—an important heads-up. While you are enjoying the blessings of having children and enjoying the good times, also prepare for the eventuality of your grown children leaving home. By developing an accurate perspective *now*, you'll be ready for your children's transition into maturity.

Sometimes moms have a hard time letting go of adult children because they've spent years cultivating a false belief of ownership. If a mom believes "This child is *mine*," she reaps a sense of abandonment when the nest empties plus reaps shame over any missteps they choose. You can sidestep these pitfalls by facing the reality right now that you don't own your children. Children are simply entrusted to you for love and for protection while they grow into becoming their own persons. Let go of possessiveness now so you'll be ready to marvel at and enjoy their maturity. When your children are grown, you'll still have your storehouse of memories.

Here's a second heads-up—good times are rarely perfect times. My children are grown now, and I'm very thankful for all the good memories. Yet I won't sugarcoat the fact that often our happy times included moments (and sometimes hours) of difficulties and challenges. For example, there was the day my children and I planned a fun celebration for their daddy. In the end we created a wonderful memory, but creating the happy memory hit major bumps along the way.

"At last!" I'd said that day. "Tonight's the night that daddy will come home from the Philippines." Remember those six weeks when I'd been left at home managing our four musketeers? Now the forty-two links had been snipped, and he was on his way home. Everyone was excited to see him, especially me. How could we give him a grand welcome?

We settled on creating a party fit for a king, calling it the King Party. I planned a kingly menu, eight-year-old John made a royal "Welcome Home" banner, and the children decorated the living room with castle decor, armor, and every knightly thing the children could imagine. We were all busy with the kingdom, a good start.

The children became more and more enthralled with the kingdom idea, having all day to invent new plans. But excitement began to give way to hassles. John tried to create a moat for the front entryway, but it didn't work and he began to complain. Three-year-old Joy tugged and pulled at me, wanting attention, but I was busy with cooking and cleaning, wanting to please my man. Little Grace needed a nap, and she began to cry.

Six-year-old Charlie had decided to mold a working goblet out of aluminum foil, a seemingly brilliant idea, but in reality Charlie was foiled by the foil. No matter how he molded or remolded it, the cup wouldn't hold water, and Charlie lost his temper. It was too much excitement and frustration to handle, even for a big six-year-old boy. My perfect day had turned into perfect chaos.

The phone rang.

"Hello?" I answered.

"Hi Rita. How's your day going? We're all so excited for Mike to get back!"

It was Libby again. What could I say? So I told her the truth.

"Awful. The kids are crabby, the party is probably ruined, and my house is still a mess. I've been trying all day just to mop the kitchen floor, but I'm going to have to pass on that idea."

"I'll be right over," she said, and in no time at all, there she was.

Libby's entrance gave the children a diversion which broke their cycle of complaint, and she added a spotless kitchen floor to our celebration. (Yay!) Meanwhile, as the girls napped, I helped my boys with the moat and the goblet, salvaging Charlie's foil creation with waterproof plastic wrap. My chaos had been transformed into hope. After accomplishing heroic exploits worthy of knighthood, Libby gave a hug and left.

That evening when Mike came through the door, he was surprised and pleased by our grand welcome home party. We sat down to a feast of meatloaf and baked potatoes, toasting him with a foil goblet of grape juice in joyful celebration. And even though the little ones were weary from excitement, we all basked in our happiness. King daddy had come home.

On New Year's Eve at the end of that year, we asked our children, "What was your favorite memory from this year?" Their reply? "The King Party for Dad!" For all of them, the party was the hands-down winner. They didn't remember the hassles at all. My takeaway: When doing fun things with children, they remember the fun. You might think hassles equal a failed event, but honestly the hassles are forgotten by the children. Their takeaway is love.

Fun celebrations with young children require a lot of effort from mom. It's hard work, but it's worth it. So give yourself a high five for all the effort you put into each and every celebration or memorable event. (And I wish I could be the friend who comes to breathe new life into your day!)

Good times, happy memories—treasures to cherish for life.

# *Seventeen*

## THE HIGH COST
## OF SACRIFICE

Are you in the whirlwind?
    Broken stuff? Interruptions to work?
        Demands from everyone? Disruptions to your sleep?
        Multilayered responsibilities at home and work?

M otherhood is much more than we ever anticipated, and its difficulties seem like huge sacrifices compared to the single life we once lived. Yet somehow love persuades us to make sacrifices, voluntarily, hoping for joy in the end. The reality that motherhood brings sacrifice hit me full force at the birth of Charlie when his heartbeat dropped and his life was in danger… and I almost lost him.

That February evening was beyond cold and icy. It was absolutely frigid. Nevertheless, we had invited Joe, a journalism student from the local university, to our house for a home-cooked meal. After supper I slipped over to the couch while Joe and Mike chatted at the table, and I began to time labor contractions. It wasn't long before I realized that this freezing night was going to be a night of birth. Our baby would be born soon.

Joe went home. Aunt Karen and Uncle Lowell arrived to take care of little John while Mike and I headed out for the big event. Mike supported my arm as I waddled across an icy street to our little Ford Fiesta, ready to navigate the bitter cold to Mercy Hospital.

Since I had chosen natural labor without an epidural, labor soon became intense. *Focus, I need to focus*, I thought. My previous childbirth classes had instructed mental focus as a way of managing pain during labor. I didn't know I would soon also need to manage the dread of losing my child. For now I just knew I needed to focus. Focus on the maroon scroll on the wallpaper. Focus on relaxation. Focus my thoughts. A verse from past readings came to mind, so I focused on Hebrews 12:2: "Jesus, for the joy set before him, endured the cross."[12]

*Jesus endured.* This phrase gave me courage. I was in pain. Jesus had experienced pain, and he understood. The pain of my labor couldn't compare to what he went through. *Try to relax and focus. Think about Jesus...*

Jesus had endured "for the joy set before him." What joy? For the joy of me. His pain was for the hopeful joy of being united with me. Jesus longed to be together forever, and so he had suffered.

A nurse came to monitor our baby's heartbeat. Not good. The heart rate was slowing a bit during contractions, and I began to feel scared, but here came another wave of pain. *Focus...*

Jesus had suffered great pain so He could offer me the gift of being declared "not guilty." He didn't come to pile on guilt (like people tend to do), but in passionate love, he had taken my guilt onto himself... for the joy set before him of being with me forever. Jesus didn't want eternal death for me; he wanted me with him!

I loved this little baby inside. For the joy set before me, I was enduring the pain. With all my heart, I wanted to see this baby, hold this wee one, and have him with me. His heart rate was still lower during contractions, and the doctor was ready to intervene if needed. Now I had to face the real possibility of a stillbirth. Terror threatened to engulf me, so I turned my focus again to Christ…

Jesus had endured excruciating pain without any guarantee that I would accept the option of being with him forever. He was willing to suffer even if he didn't receive my love in return. His love was unconditional, with no strings attached. Reciprocal love can never be commandeered, not even by God. Therefore, Jesus gave me the freedom to accept or reject his gift of being with him forever.

Though my doctor was on top of everything, I had no guarantee my baby would be born alive. And even then, I had no guarantee that he would love me someday. Children arrive without guarantees. Yet no matter what the future held, I loved him fiercely, and I would endure this and more in the days ahead for the hope of future joy.

Now I was being wheeled to the delivery room for possible intervention with forceps. Comfort was a thing of the past—we wanted to save this baby. *Focus*, I thought. *Remember the things Jesus sacrificed…*

Jesus had given up his comforts, willingly going to a sad execution to take on my punishment, a work I could barely understand. He said he could have asked the Father to send angels to rescue him, but he didn't. He endured for the joy set before him—the joy of rescuing me. Love wanted me.

Charlie's piercing cry announced his arrival. What a precious scream! My love wanted Charlie, and he was here. All my suffering had been worth it. Charlie was safe.

In the days ahead, I would have many more days of suffering, laying down my life to raise this high-spirited child. Always hopeful, I would pour out my life for my little one without any guarantee of receiving his love in return. And in retrospect thirty years later, I would do it again for each of my children, even if they chose to reject me, because I love each one. One-sided love is still love. And it is worth it all.

You will certainly suffer pain at times as you raise your challenging child. You will sacrifice comforts and pleasures in order to care for your little one. When that happens, remember that no matter what you're going through with your child, Jesus understands. He experienced all types of challenges both during his life and in his death. *Every* pain that you feel, he felt too. You can talk to him and express all your feelings because he totally gets it. What a comfort.

And while you're being comforted by Christ's empathy, also remember the reason that he was willing to suffer. It was for the *joy* of being with *you* that Jesus endured the pain of the cross. He died to give you the gift of forgiveness because he wants to be with you forever.[13] That's strong desire. Since he rose from the dead to prove that the payment for your guilt is a done deal, you can bank on his gift.[14] He is alive, so simply tell him "Thank you!" Gratitude is always a great response when you're accepting a gift!

All of us have had mommy moments that we're not proud of— moments no one else saw or moments that impacted others, worthy of apologies to kids, friends, or spouse. How wonderful it is to know that our mistakes don't spoil us for life. No need to live in the land of shame. Moreover, when we accept God's forgiveness, a new internal goodness comes to us. We receive, as a gift, the perfect purity of Christ living inside of us. God forgives, and he rebuilds our emotional damage.

God can help you with new attitudes and motives so your outside actions will spring up from that inner life within you.[15] He can help you source his patience and forgiveness in dealing with your children. He can help you love your child—the one who challenges you to the core and requires you to stand at that crossroad of sacrifice again and again. As you cultivate this desire to listen to God's perspective about living and managing your life, the results will benefit both you and everyone around you.

Amazingly, your response benefits God, too. Why? Because you bring him joy. Your smile of thanks blesses his heart. (Isn't that what we long for from our children?) Your grateful response makes his suffering immensely worth it. You *are* his joy. Is that hard for you to believe? Do you sometimes feel down, depressed, inadequate, or maybe even ashamed of hidden stuff? The antidote that sets me free from spiraling downward is remembering what Jesus has done for me out of pure love. Now I can consider myself to be pure in Christ—a gift *given* to me, not based on my own perfection.[16]

Because of Jesus Christ, God delights in us, and whenever I remember that, gratitude pops up. You are precious. You might think, "But you don't know me and all my problems." That doesn't matter. Your value isn't based on what you've done or on perfect behavior. You are intrinsically priceless just because God loves *you*.

So as you face the daily sacrifices inherent in motherhood, keep in mind the eternal picture. Remember that you're a valuable woman—a one of a kind, wonderful person whom Jesus died for so he could be with you forever. And remember that this motherhood season, which seems eternally challenging right now, will eventually disappear like a puff of smoke. In our eternity with Jesus, all of the sacrifices of today will be worth it, and all the hardships will be gone. Really!

# Eighteen

## SILVER LININGS

O ur Bergen family had finally settled into a calmer phase with routines. Now nearly five years old, Charlie was heavily into building "stuff," which kept him occupied and somewhat calm for stretches of time; John had been a quick study at reading, so his nose pointed book-ward for hours a day; and our little toddler, Joy, had not reached the strong-willed two-year-old stage yet. In addition, a young, single career woman rented one of our extra bedrooms, and since she loved to play with our kids, her presence added extra peace to our household. Grateful for the calm while she played with the children, I relaxed on our sofa, vastly pregnant. Thankful.

And unaware it was the eye of a storm.

In October baby Grace arrived, bringing all the needs of a newborn into our home. A week after Grace's birth, Joy turned two and asserted her will, strongly. Three months later we hosted a homeless lady and her son. We agreed to two weeks, but it morphed into five months. Though Charlie and John did gain a fun ten-year-old playmate, sibling rivalry soon took over, and our boys became jealous and competitive over their new friend.

Our household took on new realities: two extra ladies, an extra boy, two fighting sons, a testy two-year-old daughter, and a new baby girl. It was a new surge in the storm of life.

Yet in those months, a silver lining emerged from the dark clouds. The homeless lady took a liking to Charlie and raved over his Lego creations. With her encouragement, Charlie built an airport complex and entered it in a contest at the local department store. He won first prize—a fifty-dollar Lego Space Station.

That prize became Charlie's pride and joy, and winning the contest was a great boost to his self-confidence. The storm had brought a lady into Charlie's life who could validate his creativity with enthusiasm and encouragement. It was a wonderful silver lining, and I was grateful!

Have you ever faced excruciating days with hourly challenges? Are you in a challenging period right now? One that seems never-ending? The good news is most family-life storms pass or change. Babies grow into children who can walk to the car and strap on their own seat belts. Toddlers grow into school-age kids who can dress and feed themselves. While you wait for the storms to pass, look for the silver linings that will help you focus your thoughts on gratitude.

Did you know that research has documented many benefits from gratitude? "Be thankful" isn't just a saying. It's scientifically verified. As stated in a Harvard Mental Health Newsletter, "Gratitude helps people feel more positive emotions, relish good experiences, improve their health, deal with adversity, and build strong relationships."[17]

Research has demonstrated many benefits of gratitude,[18] such as the following:

- Improved physical and psychological health
- Enhanced sleep
- Increased self-esteem
- Reduced retaliation
- Enhanced sympathy
- Improved relationships
- Resilience from trauma (as in resilience from a colicky baby—or a cyclone!)

You can't go wrong with gratitude. So make that mental decision and choose to focus on some positive elements in any given situation. Of course you'll still be aware of the crummy stuff, but at least you'll have something positive to include in your thoughts. Go for it. Find things to be grateful for and you'll receive help and hope.

The challenges you face this year won't be the same next year. The emotional storms of life really do come and go, so hang on while you ride out this storm, and look for the silver linings.

# PART THREE

# MANAGING
# YOUR WORLD

Your Tommy has brought unique circumstances
which need to be managed, but how?
And you ask…
What's a mama to do?
Can my child learn responsibilities that will help me manage life?
Any tips for running this household?
Where can *I* find energy and refreshment?
Can I survive my active child?
Managing your own life becomes a crucial issue
while living in the world called *hyper*.

# Nineteen

## RESTED OR NOT, HERE LIFE COMES

"Choo-choo cake!" little John exclaimed while three-month-old Charlie batted at rattles and swiped at his toes.

"Let's do it!" I replied, overruling my internal debate.

*Yes, I'm exhausted and sick*, I thought, *but I **can't** ignore my son's birthday*. So in spite of nonstop coughing, I proceeded to help John craft a dream come true—a train cake for his second birthday.

Cubes of chocolate cake marched into place for coats of green icing piped with yellow swirls. (Cough.) Coal cars received loads of chocolate chips delivered by John. Hearing a cry, I sidestepped over to Charlie on the baby blanket to turn him and retrieve batted toys. (Cough, cough.) Coming back, I guided John's little fist as he piled peanuts onto the grain car. In a finishing touch, carrot wheels were placed onto each wagon, with a carrot smokestack atop the engine. (And I sniffled. And coughed.) Two candles on the cab, and we were ready to admire our work. A monumental task—accomplished!

Naptime was a must before partying. Getting the birthday boy and an active infant to sleep at the same time—while I felt lousy—presented a big challenge. While I worked at getting them down, I thought over the past twelve weeks: *What brought me to this point? Why am I this sick?*

When Charlie had arrived, John had been twenty-one months. Thankfully, my mother-in-law had traveled to assist with childcare for a week while I recovered from delivery. She'd developed a nasty cold that week, but that didn't stop her from caring for our family. Though she felt sick, I watched her press on with hard work. *I want to be like that*, I thought.

When she left, I determined I would learn how to handle this new childcare challenge. The predictable life I'd previously crafted with John had crashed to an end, so I knew I needed a new routine to handle two babies. Unfortunately, Charlie was not a routine baby. Sometimes he slept, but more often he didn't, and during the day, both boys rarely slept at the same time. At nights I awakened multiple times to the sound of my crying newborn. I became tired—no, exhausted.

But life pressed on. At the four-week mark, my good friend had a birthday. Remembering my mother-in-law's perseverance, I baked homemade bread and personally delivered it. At five weeks my husband had a business trip, so I packed up our boys and rode along to two states, staying with friends along the way. Of course Charlie's sleeping "schedule" remained erratic, and the trip didn't help. I arrived home tired—no, still exhausted.

At ten weeks some friends wanted to visit museums in Chicago. I thought of my mother-in-law and determined to take our family along on the day trip. John ogled fish at Shedd Aquarium, enthralled by motion. Mike pushed the stroller at the Chicago Field Museum. Restaurant patrons listened to Charlie's wails. We headed home after dark, and while traveling, I realized my throat had become extremely sore.

The next day John's best friend had a birthday party, and, with or without sore throat, I wanted to show our love. My mother-in-law had been sick and pushed through, so I would too. I'd forgotten that my mother-in-law had slept full nights while she'd pushed through. She wasn't staying awake at night with an inconsolable baby. *Will power can do it*, I thought. Clueless about my own body's parameters, we partied through the afternoon.

The following week I toughed it out, but my cold didn't improve and the cough got worse. Yet on Friday I couldn't resist the desire to walk my sons a mile to the local university for a Good Friday pageant. That same night, my parents arrived after their multistate drive, eager to meet their eleven-week-old grandson. I coughed my way through the weekend visit.

They left, and my cough worsened each day. But throughout that next week, I remained optimistic, remembering Mike's mother. The following Sunday brought another friend's birthday party, and now it was Tuesday, and I was prepping for John's big day. We'd already invited friends and relatives for hot dogs and train cake. I could do it!

Guests arrived.

We partied.

They left.

And John's birthday party was a grand success!

But I was not. I felt worse than ever. The following morning, the doctor confirmed I was seriously ill, so I ordered meds and went to bed. Yet my crying baby still needed to be nursed and my two-year-old son still needed care, which meant my husband had to take off work to care for the children.

Full recovery took months, but through the help of my husband and a lot of friends, we made it. At the end of that ordeal, my husband and I took a hard look at what had gone wrong. He gently helped me conclude that in the future I should be more proactive in getting enough rest, especially when sick. A body will tell you when it's exhausted. Listen.

For the sixty-eight days before our Chicago excursion, I had tried to be a superwoman. Life hadn't stopped when Charlie arrived, so I'd attempted not stopping either. Then for sixteen days after I got sick, I tried to be my mother-in-law (clueless that she'd actually been getting rest). In the end, I crashed.

I had to learn the hard way. In the future I would have to prioritize unconventional ways to find opportunities for rest because I had a nonconventional baby. Rested or not, here life comes. I would have to relearn rest in this new life or I would crash again. Not a good option. And I would need to stop living my life by comparison.

A newborn infant plus a rested mama? Does that seem like an impossibility? Of course it does. A baby in the house demands that a mommy be on the clock 24/7, nurturing your child whether you are rested or not. Adding hyperactivity to the mix doubles the challenge. Do you have a newborn in your house? Is that infant a bit colicky? Is your last full night of sleep a distant memory? If so, here's a truckload of grace from me. Don't fret that you aren't a superwoman. Just take care of Tomi, and get rest when you can.

How can you stay out of the comparison trap? By learning to be okay with your own capabilities. Whenever I compared myself with other moms, like I had done with my mother-in-law, I usually came up on the short end. So eventually I learned to stop my comparisons and my self-criticisms. It's great to learn from others, but we don't need to beat ourselves up for not being exactly like them. Each mom is a uniquely gifted lady, so let's celebrate each other, not criticize. And you can do the same and stop criticizing *yourself.*

I had to learn to be realistic about my own abilities. Some mothers have the stamina of a freight train and others of us are more like a butterfly. Each is wonderful in its own way, but each is different—which means you might need to give yourself permission to take a good look at your own abilities. Since all mothers are not alike, you'll need to discover the best way to care for your own body. When you are healthy and vibrant because of good self-care, your family will thank you. It's not selfish, but rather, in the long run, it's the best way to serve them. Be okay with taking care of your own set of needs without comparing yourself to other moms.

Also, it's okay to build margins into your schedule. If you over-schedule yourself with daily activities or outings, you don't give your body an opportunity to regroup between them. Know your own best pace and keep to it, even if it's different from your friends. Remember, a season of scaling back does not mean you are lazy.

# Twenty

## QUIET TIMES

Do you sometimes feel frazzled, without time to think? I know what you mean. Before children I'd been in the habit of taking some time every morning for a time alone—a quiet time to reflect on my circumstances, to read the Bible, and to comb my emotional tangles by thinking about God's perspective on life.

After children... impossible. (Or so it seemed.) I had to rethink the meaning of time alone to read and reflect. I had to include the *presence of children* in a new definition for *moments of solitude*.

John, our firstborn, loved to look at picture books. He could sit for long periods and "read" books, so we pursued a morning tradition we called *quiet time*. As a toddler, he would sit on a small baby quilt and look at books while I took fifteen minutes to read and reflect. I wasn't alone, but I could reflect and it worked.

Then Charlie became a toddler. I didn't want to give up quiet time, so I took my boys, the books, and the little blanket into their bedroom, shut the door, and let Charlie run around the room exploring toys while John "read" and I reflected. Thus *noise of children* was added to the *presence of children* in my *quiet time* definition, and it worked.

One morning during quiet time, eighteen-month-old Charlie took my hand and led me to a closet. Unable to talk, he pointed to a high shelf where the baby blankets lay. Translation: "I want a blanket." I handed him a little quilt and watched as he spread it beside his brother on the floor. Then he went to our bookshelf of picture books, grabbed all he could carry, and sat down on his blanket to "read," imitating his big brother. For two minutes Charlie became quiet.

That moment was an epiphany for me. Charlie had the *ability* to sit quietly. Amazing.

I contemplated the future. Was it okay to build on this newfound ability? Could I motivate him and stretch him to extend the ability? And more importantly, was this even needed? Would there ever be times when it would be good for him to know how to be quiet? I imagined the future: times in restaurants, times in doctors' waiting rooms, times on public transportation, and times where "quiet" was an asset.

Yes, this was a good and necessary skill in life, and if Charlie was going to learn "quiet," it would be best to practice it on our own turf. Springing "quiet" on him in public situations was *not* the place to begin.

Motivation was key. I'd now discovered that Charlie had intrinsic motivation to imitate his big brother. In the months ahead, by discovering other motivations, we were able to up his "quiet times" to fifteen minutes. This trained ability definitely proved useful in the years ahead.

You are not silly to wish you could have some time alone. Being a dedicated mom is a wonderful aspiration, but there may be days when you feel like you don't even have time to think. It's okay to look for ways to take care of yourself.

Since children can frazzle your brain, keep the kids safe but look for ways to give yourself the daily hug of untangling your thoughts. After all, in airplanes they ask parents to put on their own oxygen masks first and then help their children. Parents have to be alive and healthy in order to take care of their kids.

Seek creative ways to refresh: share babysitting, look for a church program, or keep on the good side of your mother-in-law! Take a look at the FAQs section at the end to get ideas for ways others can give you a boost. My friend, Lori, and I traded babysitting to help each other get a break. On days when it was my turn to care for all the children, life was as crazy as you can imagine.

Four, three, two, one, zero... *blast off*? No, this wasn't a count-down for NASA. These were the ages of five boys, and this Wednesday morning I was responsible for all five while Lori indulged in a mother's morning out. My Charlie was the one-year old at twenty-two months.

Well, in one sense it *was* a blast off—a lively morning (to say the least). The two oldest were great friends, and (when they weren't arguing) they built a tent of blankets and played camping-in-the-wilderness, complete with hunting, running, whooping, and hollering. The younger boys tried to play with their big brothers but created annoyances and destruction along the way. I supervised the action and at times distracted the younger set with singing activities, coloring books, and Duplo bricks.

All this time Lori's three-month-old baby sat quietly in his infant seat and watched his little baby hands wave in the air, stopping from time to time to doze. Did you catch that? *Sat quietly. Watched his hands. Dozed.* Every time I passed the infant seat (as I sped by while keeping up with the other four), I marveled. Remember, I had just spent the last twenty-two months with a baby who rarely sat quietly, seldom dozed, and never ever ever just sat and watched life go by. Did babies really do that? Evidently, yes. It was a nice reminder.

Meanwhile, one thought kept me energized on this busy morning: *next week I'm going out.* I would have two or three hours all alone to shop, read, or just sit and reflect. Wonderful!

The following Wednesday, I dropped off my boys at Lori's house and happily drove to the library. What a refreshment. Time alone at last.

The public library had a new book on display: *It's My Turn*, by Ruth Bell Graham.[19] Fascinated, I took the book to a cozy corner by a glass wall overlooking a garden. Settling into a stuffed chair, I traveled far away into Ruth's days of motherhood.

It hadn't been easy for her—five children and a traveling husband, and one of the children had a rebellious streak. Through perseverance and humor, Ruth had survived. Her encouragement was exactly what I needed.

Every other week, when it was my turn, I returned to the library to read that book until I'd finished it. In future weeks I chose other places to go, other things to read, or other projects to do—anything to help me unwind and refresh.

I've never ever forgotten the gracious gift Lori gave me—the gift of getting out of the house for one morning every two weeks. And I've never forgotten the courage and hope that Ruth Graham infused into my life during some of those times of going out. In fact, inspiration from her book helped motivate me to write this mommy book—for moms of the hyperactive. She survived and thrived, I survived and thrived, and so can you.

During my quiet times at home and these mornings out, I often collected Bible promises of hope. In my readings I held onto words that spoke of a positive future. For example, one of my favorite promises:

> *I would have despaired unless I had believed that I would see the goodness of the Lord in the land of the living. Wait for the Lord; Be strong and let your heart take courage; Yes, wait for the Lord.*[20]

I anchored in to this hope of God's unchanging goodness. My circumstances sometimes seemed like a mess, but the above verses reminded me that circumstances weren't the issue. My hope in God was the issue.

From promises in the Bible, I gained a bedrock that wouldn't shift in life's messy circumstances—the bedrock of God's character. Good. Loving. Life-giving. Worthy of hope. God's character became my stability in the middle of turmoil. By trusting his character, I secured my confidence that he would use the mess all around me to build *my* character into something beautiful. Instead of despairing, I could look forward to a positive future because God is good.

Quiet times. Times to refresh. Every mother's need.

# Twenty-one

## HOUSEWORK DISASTER

M anaging a super-active child is a ton of work. Running a household is also loads of work. Combine the two and there are moments when you wonder if anyone else has felt your same kind of overwhelmed. Is there anyone who recognizes how hard the work is?

Anyway, that's how I felt. When Charlie hit the stage of mobility, I hit the stage of out-of-control messy house. Actually I'd always identified more as a *messy* than a *cleanie*, but I'd made progress at keeping my stuff under control and for the most part I'd arrived. Then Charlie's arrival messed with my illusion of success. Do you remember my lament of *I don't even have time to take a vitamin*? In that phase it seemed impossible to accomplish daily chores.

On one of those insane days when my work had been interrupted by a sibling skirmish, a light bulb popped up. A sudden thought instructed me: *just finish your job*—meaning after an interruption, if possible, get back to the task at hand. This phrase stuck and became my counselor. If children interrupted my dishwashing, I would try to go back and finish the dishes rather than start a new thing. If a diaper needed to be changed while I was decluttering the countertop, I would return to decluttering. If a child's finger needed bandaging while I was opening the mail, I would try to get back to the mail to file or recycle the letters.

A couple years later, I chanced upon a book by two sisters who called themselves sidetracked home executives.[21] They'd been like me—messies by nature who had lost control of housework after kids. Their wakeup call had come when a friend observed one of their countertops scattered with soggy, used tea bags. The friend had exclaimed, "What you do is make the cup of tea and then you *throw the bag away!*"[22]

That timeless guidance matched my own previous light bulb, so my new housework motto became "Throw away the bag." I found out if I would fully complete a task at the time I was doing it, housework became a lot more manageable.

Now by "manageable," I don't mean easy. No way. The onslaught of housework marched forward, and I usually felt behind. I added an infant to my five-year-old son plus my three-year-old hyperactive boy, and the sum of that calculation equaled a housework disaster. While I seemingly made progress in one room, the kids could undo other rooms faster than I could keep up. No matter how long and hard I worked, I couldn't keep my own standards. Maybe my standards were too high or maybe too low, but often I didn't meet them—which equaled mommy disaster. I was a failure in the housework department according to… me, which created in me a disaster of discouragement.

On one of those days, I was working in the kitchen while baby Joy relaxed in her stroller beside me (safe from her hyper-brother). I rushed through my chores, scrubbing the breakfast dishes and loading some laundry (simultaneously, of course) so I could nurse the baby ASAP. Suddenly my ears were filled with the sound of a mess. Yes, the *sound*. Having heard that distinctive tone of laughter before, I instinctively knew it meant my boys were up to no good. Haven't you experienced that dreaded sound? You know!

Racing around the corner and down the hall, I saw it—disposable diapers and toilet paper flying out of the bathroom to squeals of delight (from the children of course, not from me!). So even though my kitchen was clean, the bathroom was now trashed. How and why did these two little boys decide to do home decorating with diapers and toilet paper? Why did they choose this moment for a creative streak?

Forget the laundry. My next job was laid out for me—it was time to clean the bathroom. The boys helped pick up and clean up, but it required supervision, so it completely changed the goals I'd set for the morning. The housework goals would have to wait for another day while I helped my boys learn responsibility for messes (as I tried to remind myself that *teaching* them was important work, too).

During those crazy days, my ever-compassionate mother-in-law said, "Trying to clean the house with young children around is like trying to shovel snow during a snowstorm. As long as the snow is still falling, it won't look like you've done much—no matter how hard you work."

Have you ever shoveled snow *during* a snowstorm? Feels pretty fruitless. You work hard and become exhausted, but the flakes keep coming and the wind keeps blowing, and it's hard to see any progress. That's how my work felt—no progress. Yet in reality, a partly shoveled walk will require less shoveling later, every snowstorm is temporary, and every winter is merely a season that will pass. Likewise, my work did accomplish a bit of maintenance (however small), and eventually a new season of life eliminated unmanageable disorder. Just like a snowstorm, the housework disaster eventually passed and—surprise—became paired with precious memories.

Have you noticed by now that many of my frustrations came from interruptions? Do disruptions hinder all your well-laid plans, too? Yet children, by nature, *are* interrupters. They have immediate needs with no cognizance of our deadlines. My sister-in-law, Karen, once found a great quote about interruptions that helped me. That quote simply said, "Interruptions are my work." Because of this quote, I came to view my children's problems and needs differently. On busy days of caring for children, the quote reframed my thinking. The children were not interruptions to my work, but rather their needs *were* my work. Some additional advice helped, too. A friend admonished, "Take care of one thing at a time, and then go on to the next." Great advice. Just focus on the interruption needing attention right now and manage that moment.

Thankfully, over time I also came to realize that in and of itself, a clean house is not the ultimate goal. It's merely a means for reaching the real goal—that of loving your family. At the end of the day, you measure success differently than by a clean house. "Did I show love today? Did I instruct my children in wisdom about life? Did I pray for them?" You have succeeded! Remember, if you had a different job with work that stayed done, even the so-called lasting work doesn't last forever. So in each moment, just do the next thing that needs to be done, and remind yourself that building the character of children is more consequential than any other job on earth.

All children bring full-time work. Childcare plus household care takes overwhelming effort. We comrades of motherhood understand. Though a hyperactive child appears to bring you more work, in reality all mothers give constant effort in caring for every kind of child, just in different ways. So get ready to persevere through the day, ready to put one foot in front of the other. Every mountain can be climbed one step at a time. You'll get through this season, and the work you do now will be totally worth it all.

# Twenty-two

## SHOPPING

"One, two, three—jump!" I called cadence while boosting four-year-old Charlie into the seat of the grocery cart. It wasn't easy heaving a thirty-pound boy. And with me being newly pregnant (fourth time), I wasn't feeling all that great. But since it would be worse if Charlie were running loose in the store, I built my muscles through heaving.

Charlie sat in one cart, toddler Joy sat in another, and six-year-old John walked behind. Heads turned and people made way as I pushed one cart and pulled the other. My train of two carts wove its way through tall shelves stocked with bottles and boxes. By steering to the center of the aisle, little fingers couldn't pull items off the shelf.

"Can we get macaroni and cheese?" "Why does that man have his hat on backward?" "I don't want applesauce!" "I want the cereal with the toy telescope." "He hit me!" "Can we get macaroni and cheese?" "I want to get out and look at the cereal." "Can we get some macaroni and cheese?"

*If only they wouldn't ask so many questions, I could think what I needed.* "Charlie, stop kicking the grocery cart!" *Sigh.*

Every week I went to the store, pushing and pulling two carts, each filled to the brim. The routine turned into a never-ending circle: take food off the grocery shelves, into the cart, onto the conveyor belt, into the car, into the house, onto cupboard shelves, and into little tummies. Back to the store next week, two carts again, busy children, 'round the store, into the car, and back home. Store, home, store, home.

The never-ending cycle of groceries gave a never-ending challenge of shopping with a hyperactive child in tow. Our road-runner-in-the-china-store problem needed creative solutions. Two carts was my solution for years. I'm sure people wondered why such a big boy was sitting in the grocery wagon and why such a petite ninety-eight-pound mother would bother to lift him in. But we had our reasons, and it worked. Never mind what other people thought; they would've had much worse thoughts if I had let him walk (run!) in the store.

Shopping with any child is a challenge. Children don't under-stand property issues (the items for sale belong to the store, not us). They don't have a concept of polite store manners (don't touch). They don't comprehend budget constraints (no, that's too expensive). They haven't polished their public behavior, throwing protests of fury for items they want (insert blush of shame here). Shopping brings a big learning experience for any child, which adds to the work for mom. Then hyperactivity doubles that work. On top of everything, besides teaching your children these lessons in maturity, you have an impor-tant agenda to accomplish—you need to get this errand done before the next meal—but they don't understand the concept of deadline. A shopping challenge for the mom? That's an understatement.

When planning to shop with an extra-active child, creative

solutions become the key. You have a problem, and you have a brain. Name the problem (e.g., Charlie will break pickle bottles), and brainstorm a solution (e.g., If Charlie sits in the grocery cart, he is restrained from touching everything).

Also, while you're dealing with the need for a solution, please remember that children's feelings are fragile. When shopping, don't hurl personal accusations at them, such as "you stress me out!" This type of attack on their personhood only "works" by crushing them, and that's a terrible option. Put-downs don't really resolve problems but rather create new (deeper) issues. Instead of insulting Tomi, you can simply acknowledge the obvious and say, "We have a problem, and we need to look for solutions." This acknowledges the problem as an objective issue outside of both of you, a problem that can be worked on together.

Meanwhile, it's good to acknowledge that a shopping trip is *effort*. So give yourself an A+ every time you take your children to the store. Even if you come home without any purchases and you feel like your trip was a failure—your effort was awesome!

# Twenty-three

## THE BIG PICTURE

Looking at the framed photo collage on my wall, my heart felt that familiar squeeze of love, and I reminisced. I saw the photo of young John posed beside his chalkboard, proud of his stickman drawing of daddy. I could practically hear baby Grace squealing—a picture of happiness as she lay kicking on the comforter of my bed. Joy's dimples grinned back at me from her pose beside her siblings, and little Charlie smiled from ear to ear, ready to blow out the three candles on his merry-go-round cake. This collage on my wall framed memories from eight years of mothering. Charlie, though at times seemingly all consuming, was just one photo in the big picture of my life.

The phone rang. A phone interruption was actually pretty common in my life's picture. As the primary assistant for my husband's business, I did a lot of phone answering.

"Hello," I responded.

"I'm wondering if you can help us," said the voice on the other end. "We need some money for groceries."

*Oh,* I thought. *This is probably legit, but he might be a scammer. What do I do?*

Quickly assembling my thoughts, I replied, "I'm sorry to hear that. I'll let my husband know, and he can get back with you." I knew this call was way beyond me to figure out, so I tossed the ball into my husband's court. Whew.

That taken care of, I glanced at the clock and realized it was past time to start baking cookies for tonight's meeting in our home. Even though my husband had an office, he often used our house as a base of operations because I enjoyed hosting. Functioning as his assistant was my part-time job, or maybe full-time, depending on the season. So I scooted two chairs to the kitchen counter for my little girls to help measure flour and stir sugar (and snitch chocolate chips). While we baked, Charlie drew whales and dolphins at the kitchen table, which I hoped would occupy him until I could give personal attention to his kindergarten lesson. I trusted John could stay interested in his reading workbook while I multitasked my jobs of chief cook, home educator, and administrative assistant.

I was not just a mom of a hyperactive child, but also a busy mother with a full life. Can you relate? I was creating multiple memory albums, not just a photo collage, and you are, too. You have a super-active child, yet you have a whole life to live. Maybe you juggle work and home responsibilities, giving it your all on the job, yet coming back to a house that greets you with work undone (while Tommy creates more). Maybe you have more than one child, which means multiple needs to meet; or needy parents who demand your attention; or committee meetings for the neighborhood watch, not to mention your desire to help your sick friend by dropping off a meal; or spending an afternoon at the mall with cousins. Hyperactivity is just one of the many balls you juggle—children, friends, work, church, and more.

Like me, the juggled balls often include multiple children. In my busy life of caring for a high-spirited child, it was possible to neglect the needs of the others. I purposely had to carve out time for helping John plant his garden and time for reading picture books to Joy and Grace. My super-active child required lots of attention, so I had to evaluate what kinds of attention the others needed. That's true for you, too. Look for ways to affirm each of your children to let them know they are important to you. Since every child *is* equally important, intentionally make time to focus on each child.

My big picture included not only responsibilities with my children and tasks for my husband, but also friendships. Every Wednesday evening, Aunt Karen, Uncle Lowell, and their kids joined us for food, fun, and friendship. My girlfriends and I went on outings with our children: a children's farm, the city park, and a local mall. Another friend group picnicked at lakes, camped together at the state park, and toured Chicago's museums. Friendships are important in your big picture. You can either stay isolated and ingrown with your hyperactive child, or you can look for ways to be involved with friends.

My photo collections also included church memories. Our church helped local university students transition from youth into adulthood, and I gladly welcomed these students to home-cooked meals and conversations about life. (Remember Joe from the night of Charlie's labor and delivery? Yes, Joe was definitely in our memory albums.) We also received international students from Mali, China, and the Philippines to temporarily live in our home while they looked for permanent housing.

And throughout all this, the phone kept ringing…

"Hello," I answered once again.

"Hi, Rita." I recognized the voice of my husband's supervisor.

"Could you have Mike get in touch with me? A partner organization in the Philippines needs someone to move over to Manila to help them. Because of your experience with Filipino students at the university, I thought of you and Mike. Can you have Mike call me?"

Move our family to Manila in the Philippines? Outlandish? Exciting? Either way it was a huge fork in the road to consider. My jaw basically hit the floor.

But on the other hand, moving overseas was not out of the question for me because in the big picture, my husband and I had always been dreamers. Even before marriage we'd discussed the possibility of an overseas stint someday, and having a hyperactive child didn't erase our dreams. Charlie was a major photo in our big picture, but hyperactivity didn't determine destiny. Marriage partnership remained a primary photo, and our marriage dreams stayed in the frame.

In making the decision, many factors entered into our discussions, including the state of my health plus the needs of Charlie and our other children. In the end we concluded that if we were ever going to pursue our international dream, now, before our kids' teen years, was the best time. So the dreams that had been laid aside became activated, and we relocated to Metro Manila for a year.

Have your dreams been laid aside, seemingly tattered or obliterated by the whirlwind? Do you dare even hope to keep big visions in your big picture? Though reality always reigns supreme, you never know when hope's dreams might get called up by an opportunity. In the meantime, you can leave your hopes at the feet of your heavenly father in prayer. Destiny is his business.

All these photos created a large picture for my life. Snapshots in memory albums and on my wall represented years packed with dear people and memorable moments. The events in Charlie's life didn't happen in a vacuum. Though Charlie was super-active and required lots of care, he was only one event in our family. I loved him dearly and was dedicated to his progress, but that was true of every child in our family—and actually of lots of people in my life. Managing Charlie was merely part of the bigger picture of managing my world.

# Twenty-four

## MORAL FOUNDATIONS

I relaxed in bed, reflecting on the day's events. Charlie had been busy that day, really this whole past month, getting ready for this night of celebrating four years of high school—prom night. A tux had been rented, hair had been cut, a corsage bought for a lovely young lady, and prom tickets purchased for a banquet and dance. Charlie's friend group had made plans to party together. One of the gals in that group had agreed to play the part of Charlie's "date" (hence the corsage), but in reality they were all just a group of friends going to prom together, not a date thing. The group had pooled their scant dollars to rent a limousine and fund an after-party at one of their homes. These teens had already proved to be good friends to Charlie, and I hoped they were having a good time.

I laid in bed thinking how proud I was that Charlie had thought ahead to make all those arrangements, overcoming his scatterbrain tendencies to get everything done on time. Still awake, I heard a key turn in the door lock after midnight, and Charlie tiptoed into the quiet house. (Yes, of course I was awake. Do mothers ever fall asleep quickly when their child is out with a party crowd?) I rose to inquire, "Why such an early arrival?" And the story unfolded.

The trip to a neighboring city had been great fun, a once-in-a-lifetime limousine ride for these kids of moderate means. They'd feasted on banquet food at a fancy hotel, listened to booming music in the dance hall, and even ventured onto the dance floor (though prom-style dancing wasn't Charlie's forte). As the party had wound down, Charlie's friend group had piled into the limo for the forty-five-minute trip back to the house of one of the group for their all-night after-party (which was why Charlie's "early arrival" had surprised me).

While the kids had traveled, they'd discussed and joked about their plans for the evening, plans, Charlie discovered, that included alcohol. And some planned to drink till inebriated, or so they'd said. Charlie had listened. And contemplated. And decided.

Charlie didn't want to get drunk. Charlie didn't even want to be around drunk friends. So Charlie had made the gutsy decision to ask the limo driver to drop him off at our house, which was on the way to the party house. Since this party was really a group event more than a date event, the girl he'd escorted wouldn't exactly be abandoned—she was still part of the group. So Charlie came home.

An unexpected fork in the road had presented itself, and Charlie had chosen the high ground. I was extremely proud of Charlie!

I never heard whether individuals at the party ended up drunk, and I didn't feel a need to inquire. Maybe they changed their minds, or maybe it had all been trash talk. But no matter, the important thing was Charlie had perceived danger and made his choice. He hadn't impulsively joined a crowd in revelry, but rather he'd chosen the fork in the road labeled "Sobriety." On this night, his conscience had triumphed over impulsiveness, which gave me assurance that Charlie was ready for adulthood. To maturity and beyond!

Like me, perhaps you worry about all the dangers and temptations your child will face as they navigate the future. You and I know it can be scary out there. Every mom wonders, *Will my child survive?* And when you have a child prone to impulsiveness, it's enough to make your fingernails disappear. But think about this: Do you remember things your mother warned you about? Or cautions from another caregiver? Of course you do. Their words can echo in your mind for life. A son will continue to hear his mom's admonishment to "Play it safe," even when his mother is in the grave. So be encouraged. Your children will hear the recording of your voice during the dangerous times ahead. Maybe someday they will even give you a hug and say, "Mom, you were right!"

Managing your world includes giving your kids a moral foundation, not only preparing them to survive the present but also to survive the future. You can't control that future world, but you do presently manage your input into those days to come. Through diligent teaching today, you give your children a mental collection of audio recordings they can draw on when they face temptations ahead. By dialoguing with them about current dilemmas, you help them develop critical thinking for upcoming forks in the road.

How can you input recordings into your child's mind that will replay in the future? Discover the secret of the recording studio in your home. Children's minds absorb their parents' words, even when they aren't yet responding positively. Recordings happen daily, automatically. By giving your children truths about the world around them, you load them up with "Podcasts from Mom."

Often we give simple commands without explanations, expecting the child to obey just because we told them. That's good, and they should trust us moms. But it misses a bigger opportunity—that of capitalizing on the opportunity to give the moral reasons behind the commands. A prime opportunity for stocking a child's mind with moral information is whenever you give an instruction of any kind. This bite-sized moral lesson will be of immense help to them in future situations. Of course, you can't do this *every* time you give a command because of time constraints, but by explaining ethics and values whenever you can, you'll help your child for life.

For example, one evening you say, "Tommy, come mop the kitchen floor." That's good, and Tommy should do it just because you're the mom and you want what's best for him. But if you take the simple instruction deeper and explain the reasons behind your instruction, you're adding to the podcasts in his mind, such as the following:

"Tommy, I need you to mop the kitchen floor tonight. I know you want to play video games, and you can do that after the floor is clean. Tonight your sister has a cold, so she can't do her normal chores. Our family shows compassion and helps people when they have a problem."

This takes some extra time, but when you give your child the good reasons for your instruction, you build their trust toward you as well as increase their motivation to obey. Though Tommy may still resist you in the moment, your reasons will stick with him for years (even when he doesn't remember where he learned all he knows). Giving moral reasons for your instructions is worth your time—and theirs.

Another way to help your children with future forks in the road is to give them some age-appropriate freedoms. Then help them think through various ways they might choose to use that freedom and the probable consequences of each option. Discussing the pros and cons of choices helps your child develop discernment and wisdom. It's good to do this while they are still at home and you are with them.

The alternative is for you to withhold freedoms and remain a control freak for eighteen years, making every decision for your child. Then at eighteen when they receive legal freedom, you'll have to release them to the sharks of this world without any tools for discernment. Horrors!

Through this dual strategy of giving moral explanations plus dialoguing about free choices, you'll give your children the moral compass they need for navigating adulthood. Manage your words wisely now, and they'll reap wisdom for life.

# Twenty-five

## SQUIRT SOME LAUGHTER

The summer sun beckoned my preschool boys, enticing them to the backyard for a romp in hot weather, providing a good outlet for hyperactive muscles. As I stood in the shade supervising my laughing children, I felt a bit of nostalgia. Oh, to be a child again. Running in the grass. Laughing. Playing.

*Look at all that fun,* I thought.

Then a light bulb: *I can join them, and we can laugh together!*

But reality hit: *Look at all that heat.*

A sudden brainstorm united my two desires—fun and comfort—into one grand plan. I grabbed some squirt toys from the house and ran out to join the fun. "Let the games begin!" The boys were thrilled for mommy to join the laughter.

Squirt and squirt!     Squirt, squirt, squirt
      Run through grass     Laugh and play
Chuckling boys   Gleeful shrieks   Giggle, giggles   Water trickles
Squirt... and squirt!     Squirt, squirt, squirt
      Run and hide         Sneak up slow
            Sprint so fast       Faster, fast!
Dripping mom   Swipe the face   Wipe the eyes   Duck around
      Squirt the boys         Boys squirt back
Squirt and squirt!     Squirt, squirt, squirt!


We frolicked in the sun till we were all dripping wet. And then we ran some more, oblivious to the clock in the kitchen. Suddenly I heard a voice behind me.

"Hi, Rita!"

My friend, Lori, was calling out as she came through the backyard gate. Since she just lived a few blocks away, she'd decided to drop off some things at my house.

"Hi, great to see you!" I said, water dripping from my eyelashes and tousled hair.

"I knocked on your front door," she explained. "No one answered, but I heard all this laughter in the distance, so I came around to see if it was you."

"Oh yeah, no problem. I'm glad you felt free to come find us." And I added, "I hope you don't mind that I'm dripping wet. We were just having a little fun." (Duh, that was obvious.)

"Oh, no that's fine," she replied. "I wish I played with my boys like this more often. I need to make more time for laughing with them."

Those words echoed in my own mind for years to come, reminding me to make time to laugh together with my children. I became intentional about allowing and bringing laughter into the home. Laughter and smiles and family fun—a language of love.

Laughter is medicine. You need a good dose of it every now and then to keep your equilibrium. Do you remember laughing as a child? It's good to laugh now, too. It's not just children who need laughter. You do as well—which might be enough to make you cry at that thought. But take heart. Laughter lives somewhere deep down, just waiting to erupt. If it's been a long time since you have felt like laughing, that's okay. A time of grief can be acknowledged. But laughter is just around the corner when you're ready to gather the courage to look for it.

In every home, healthy laughter is also good for the child's soul. I'm not talking about the kind of laughter that's at the expense of others, belittling them or laughing to their shame. But I mean a good old-fashioned chuckle from finding humor in life and cherishing light-hearted moments.

When families play together (without turning every game into competitive one-upmanship), the ensuing giggles can be glue for the whole. Our family wasn't perfect at this, but we intentionally carved out weekly time for family fun and togetherness. It didn't take money, just creativity. We designed indoor golf games. We created restaurants in the bedrooms, ate picnics at a river, and flew pretend airplanes in the den. The sky's the limit for fun ideas. Get ideas from friends, or browse the Internet, or check out game books from the library. Find fun for your family.

Also, if possible, find some friends who will laugh with you at the humorous moments of mothering. Raising kids can be hilarious at times if you don't take everything too seriously. While I was writing this section, I got the following group text from a mommy friend. It reads:

# Today's Edition of "Why Is This Wet?"

Me: Why are these clay flowers all wet?

Two-year old [who doesn't actually talk yet]: Because mama, you were busy teaching sister reading, so I decided it was a fabulous idea to climb up on the table and drop them all into sister's milk that she left here for me to find even though you thought I was happily playing downstairs with brother. Oh, and I spilled the mug of milk too, just in case you didn't notice.

Me: I see.[23]

No kidding, this text arrived while I was writing this section. *This mom knows how to reach out to friends and laugh*, I thought. Notice she started by saying, "Today's Edition of 'Why Is This Wet?'" She acknowledged the reality of *daily* surprises from immature kids, and she chose to share her shock with friends to let them find humor with her. We can either laugh or cry (or yell) about frustrations with immature children. Sometimes it's best to laugh by telling the frustration to a friend who can help you lighten up.

Go after some smiles and laughter, moms. It's good for your soul and helps your family to thrive. Let go and laugh!

# Twenty-six

## SCHOOL DAYS,
## WORRY DAYS

It's hard to instruct a bundle of energy (at least hard to teach "book learning"), and when other children or siblings outpace your Tomi, it's tempting to compare her to them and panic.

Like my temptation to compare Charlie with our first child, John. John learned to read at age five, catching on naturally. By six he was off and running, reading books like *Little House on the Prairie*. But when Charlie was five, he was a bullet that stopped occasionally to build cities and space stations. He didn't sit to listen to a book being read to him, much less try to learn to read one himself. I was a little worried about his education. How do you teach a bullet?

We had decided to homeschool our kids through their early years (public school later), so I was able to create a customized plan for Charlie's kindergarten. He was active, so kinesthetic learning experiences were just the ticket—eye–hand coordination, sequences of patterns, plus some simple arithmetic and the alphabet. I tried to teach him phonics, but he didn't get it. I became a little worried. By now his seven-year-old brother could read three *The Hardy Boys* books a week.

During Charlie's first grade year, I reasoned, "If I sit with Charlie *every day* to help him practice reading, surely he'll be reading by the end of the year." Not so. At the end of a year, he was no more ready to read than he'd been at the beginning. Hours of practice didn't make a dent. By now his brother was reading biographies and encyclopedias.

Throughout Charlie's second grade year, I continued working with him on phonics and simple words but with little progress. Yet amazingly, he developed into a math whiz. His brother (who by now was reading at high school level) struggled with his fourth grade math. I began to get perspective.

Two children, two different sets of abilities, and two different needs in learning style. When it came to education, being unique was okay.

Charlie was unique. Though math made sense to him, in second grade he still had trouble focusing long enough to accomplish an entire math workbook page. While working on assignments, he stood up, he sat down, and sometimes he looked like a boxer punching his way to victory. Charlie needed multiple breaks to survive second and third grades. It was fourth grade before he settled down and listened to a read-aloud chapter book for the first time, a historical fiction book I was reading to my girls. The other children had enjoyed read-aloud books from, well, almost from birth. Not Charlie. But that was okay. Though Charlie learned at his own pace and in his own style, he *did* learn. In third grade he began to catch up to his grade level in reading. I didn't need to compare.

Education can be a big worry for moms. The hyperactive child often has some learning differences and also a unique learning style.

This means you will need to be Tommy's advocate in education. Embrace that reality. Educate yourself on the various learning styles of children (e.g., info about learning-style profiles at cynthiatobias.com/resources-2/resources/[24]). Talk to Tomi's teachers or guidance counselors, and persevere in finding a learning environment that will help her thrive. The school's job is to assist parents in discovering ways to educate Tommy and Tomi. Also, don't shy away from considering possibilities outside the box. For example, home education for hyperactive children was an option suggested by some experts, and it worked for us. Explore all of your options.

Always remember, if Tommy doesn't learn it this year, there's always next year. Many children catch up in academics (though not all are able). In the meantime, stay focused on developing your child's character because learning respectful attitudes will take him far in life.

# Twenty-seven

## ROUTINE EXPECTATIONS

"Tea will be ready in five minutes," I announced to no one in particular but everyone in general.

Joy scurried to brush her hair as ten-year-old Charlie rolled out of bed, rubbing his eyes. In five minutes the whole family would be gathered in the family room to start our day with family teatime, a morning together-time—routinely expected.

Each day we read together, then discussed what we learned, and gathered memories. (Ah, teatime memories. You can ask me sometime about the day a pet mouse jumped out of Joy's hand during our teatime and our whole family had to race to the rescue or the times tea spilled onto laps or books. There's a tea stain on a book to prove it.)

Routines. Expectations. Less frenzy. Since each day we ate breakfast right after teatime, the children expected to go straight from the family room to the kitchen. After breakfast each child completed a prescribed daily chore. Routinely. They worked on their school lessons at a certain, expected time.

Charlie knew the prescribed place for dirty clothes (in a basket under a basketball hoop… swish and score!) and the designated boxes for his Legos (under the Lego building table).

Each Saturday morning, a Pine-Sol scent wafted throughout the house and our vacuum cleaner roared. Our children had already been given a choice as to their preferred chores, and now they were expected to help clean the house together.

And always, bedtime was a given (though the prescribed time advanced with age). Putting on pajamas, brushing teeth, bedtime prayers, and "Goodnight, I love you!"

These and other habitual practices became a gift—both to Charlie and to me. By this time I had read a lot of info about hyperactivity. "Have a clear routine for the child," advised the US Department of Health and Human Services.[25] Their advice was given to help the child, but in reality it also helped me.

When Charlie knew what to expect, I didn't have to deal with as many attention deficit issues. (No need to "listen" when you already know.) When customary practices were followed, I didn't have to deal with the outbursts caused by Charlie hearing unexpected directives. (Fewer surprises equaled fewer reactions.) Having daily and weekly routines calmed Charlie's behavior, containing the disarray.

"Where do I begin?" you might be asking. When life has been chaotic, everything can seem overwhelming, including the establishment of new customs. You might think the picture I described is impossible for your Tommy. But pause and realize that this snapshot of teatime with Charlie and our family was *years* down the road. The customs had been established in increments, not all at once.

Making schedules and establishing routines sound like work, right? It *is* work. But in reality, not having routines also means work.

You have to work at getting your children to cooperate. You have to slog through a life lived in disorder. Either way, you will work. So I concluded the work of teaching my children to follow routines would be beneficial and worth it—helping me now and benefitting my children both now and later.

If you feel overwhelmed right now at the thought of establishing routines, I hear you. But please don't despair. Routines aren't your master. They are your servants, so don't feel enslaved by the thought. Just whenever you feel ready, start one new habit for your family, however small, and later add another. The benefits will build over the years. And by the way, you would be right if you guessed that we didn't always follow our own routines. Daily, weekly, and monthly fluctuations happened regularly. For sure. Our family was routinely flexible because routines were not the master. They were established to serve the family.

When you are ready to establish new routines, I highly recommend the use of rewards. Don't just punish your children into a new system. Incentivize. To start a new practice, I always began with the end goal in mind (such as "We need weekly housecleaning"). Then I looked for ways to motivate toward that goal. I looked at it from the child's point of view and brainstormed incentives (knowing that in the end, *I* would be rewarded by the routine).

Here's an example of one of our incentives: Most children aren't intrinsically motivated to clean a house. Yet it's a skill that will benefit them both now and later. So I used the motivation of letting them choose between necessary jobs. "Would you rather dust the living room or clean the bathroom?" I also motivated them by promising they could read the Saturday comics after chores were all done. Believe it or not, this reward worked for my kids, but you'll have to find your own motivators—the ideas that work for your gang. There are many methods of motivation, and whole books have been written on great ways to motivate children.

You can do it, not perfectly, of course, but enough that your whole family will receive the benefit—including your active one.

# Twenty-eight

## GETTING ORGANIZED

I tiptoed around clutter strewn from Charlie's backpack and sat on the sofa beside him, careful not to displace papers in the scattered piles. This mess signified Charlie's first day of high school, and the mess was waiting for my signature on dozens of those papers. I looked over supply lists and syllabi, signing to confirm I was aware of each class's requirements.

Freshman year in high school meant a new chapter for Charlie's life. His math-whiz capabilities had enabled him to test into a science and technology program at a magnet school outside our regular district. But this scholastic achievement brought an onslaught of new and extra-challenging responsibilities. Since Charlie had attention deficit tendencies, Charlie needed to get organized!

After the second day of school, Charlie and I traipsed to the local discount store to rummage through shelves of three-ring binders and notebook dividers. Each class required separate notebooks and dividers, so we needed six sets. Whew, that would mean a loaded backpack with all those notebooks and textbooks. Those science and engineering classes were obviously going to accomplish more than academics. They were going to build physical strength. And they were going to teach a life skill—organization.

Charlie and I filled the cart with other needed items. We decided that a portable three-hole punch was mandatory equipment for this paper venture. Into the cart it went, along with a compass and a higher-function calculator, plus all the paper and pencils a student would need. Charlie and I carted his supplies home and started organizing.

By the third day, assignments were pouring in. Thankfully, Charlie's high school had gifted each student with a daily planner. I took a glance and discovered a custom printed guide which included a calendar of school events on each week's page plus some tips for students. The daily squares on the calendar gave ample room for jotting assignments, listing exam dates, and noting project deadlines. By now Charlie's planner was beginning to show third-day wear of penciled words and scribbled dates—meaning he already had some deadlines to meet. Organization kicked in!

Fourth and fifth days came, and I watched my previously scatter-focused son use these new tools to remember assignments and meet deadlines. This high school had nailed down a system for helping every student succeed. I was grateful. Charlie got organized.

It's not uncommon to need to spend extra effort at teaching responsibility to an energetic, unfocused child. A scattered brain often comes with the territory of hyperactivity (which is enough to make your own brain scatter). Caring for your *own* responsibilities is more than enough to manage, but now you have a child who seems to need supervision every step of the way, and that can tip you into frustration.

Just remember, the absentminded child may be in the

embryonic stage of something great because the absentminded child has a very present mind—for whatever she is thinking about. Take heart. Scatterbrained children really do have a brain.

Meanwhile, unfocused children need help learning to manage their own lives. Your role is to support and teach them as they hit walls because of needing more structure. Charlie's high school had tools for teaching students how to get organized. Likewise, many books are available with organizational helps for your child, and websites exist with ideas for supporting the needs of the hyperactive (e.g., multiple articles listed on the Organizing Your Child menu at ADDitudemag. com[26]).

Resources can offer ideas both for now and also for the future when they, as adults, will need organizational skills—paying bills, keeping jobs, and even wooing a mate. Since you won't be with them forever to do everything for them, you must help them discover techniques for managing their own lives. Your job is to inspire your child to pursue resources that can help him, but every child is different, so motivate your Tommy toward discovering how to manage his own world.

# Twenty-nine

## NAVIGATING FAILURE

"Hello, Mrs. Bergen?" A ringing phone had interrupted my peace (again).

"This is Charlie's Spanish teacher."

"Oh, hi," I replied (though honestly my internal reply was, *Oh no!*).

"I'm calling to let you know that Charlie is close to failing Spanish this quarter. He hasn't been turning in assignments, and his grade is falling."

I cringed at this unexpected and unwelcome news.

She continued, "Charlie isn't a bad student, but right now he is shooting himself in the foot."

Wow, whoa. What can a mom say to that?

"Thanks for letting me know. I'll talk to Charlie."

I hung up the phone and sighed. The end of winter had morphed into spring. I had thought Charlie was on a downhill cruise to high school graduation, but evidently not. A failing grade didn't bode well for graduation. Actually I'd sort of noticed that Charlie had been acting differently this final semester of his senior year, but I'd chalked it up to "senioritis" and had considered it sort of "normal." But now I needed to face the reality of his neglect.

The past few years, Charlie had learned to work hard in high school. He'd learned to organize notebooks and follow his daily planner and study his lessons. He'd succeeded at getting to the bus stop on time. He'd stayed up late to complete homework assignments, and he'd received a slew of good grades over the course of his high school career. I was very proud of his efforts, especially considering this was the child I'd once agonized over because of his lack of reading!

And now this. What?

The "what?" needed to be answered by Charlie. We had our talk, and he realized the gravity of failure. Failing to turn in assignments could lead to a failing grade, which could lead to failure to graduate, which could result in failure to gain access to his university of choice. His present choices would impact choices for the future.

Whenever a child fails at something important, we moms groan and (inwardly) exclaim, "NO-O-O-O!" Mothers don't want pain for their children, and since failure brings pain, a child's anguish is hard to watch. If you are in that situation right now with a child, I feel for you.

Success is never a certainty in life. The attainments we want for children will sometimes be hard to come by. I wish I could cushion this harsh reality of life, but like it or not, failure is a part of everyone's existence. All children will face it at some point in their lives. Because of this, it's good to help children view present failures as opportunities to learn. Failure can be a blessing in disguise.

First, failure teaches the laws of sowing and reaping. When failures have arrived because of a child's own irresponsibility, they need to feel the pain they've brought upon themselves. To help your children learn important lessons, set boundaries for yourself against rescuing them from failure. You cannot help your children learn about reaping what they sow if you always step in to rescue them from pain. As mentioned before, in your responsibility to teach and train your children, you have a role—to empathize with the pain they've brought on themselves and give advice about their next steps. But you are not responsible for their own choices. They own that responsibility. Though pain is hard to watch, don't take all that pain away if it came as a result of their own decisions. Let them learn. This is your responsibility in helping them mature.

Secondly, failure can force children to learn the source of their true value. Since failure often challenges a child's sense of worth, it forces them to discover their own intrinsic worth apart from "success." They learn that love, from both you and God, is not based on the successes they've achieved but rather on their created value.

Lastly, in failure children learn courage and responsibility. It takes courage to pick yourself up after failure, and it takes responsibility to move forward even while knowing that the new steps might not succeed. It takes courage to face personal fears, and it takes responsibility to own those fears and confront them.

On a side note, I used to wonder, "Where does mercy fit into this? Can't I rescue them from pain because I'm a loving, merciful mom?" A helpful answer came from a conference by Dr. Henry Cloud. He advised that if a child is normally responsible but has an occasional lapse, it's certainly appropriate and merciful for you to come to the rescue. But if your child has a pattern of irresponsibility in an area, that child needs to feel some pain to learn he reaps what he sows. In a situation of irresponsibility, continual "mercy" is not a loving response because you short-circuit the opportunity to mature. So even though it feels loving, it's not really love. Is that answer helpful to you? I know it certainly helped me.

Watching children go through failure can be an emotional time for moms (especially if it has come from that child's own bad choices). While your child goes through the trauma of failure, their ordeal can feel like your own. Unfortunately, these feelings won't get any easier when they are adults. The stakes just become higher. Romances fail. Jobs are lost. Cars get totaled. The grief of an adult child will often hit the mom hard, so courage and responsibility are key once again—for you.

Since it doesn't get easier when a child is grown, right now is the time for you and your child to learn how to go through failure. Right now is their opportunity to internalize the lessons of how to fail. Right now is your opportunity to model and teach attitudes of courage and responsibility. Right now is also your opportunity to let go of possessiveness, refusing to view them as merely an extension of yourself. Their failure does *not* equal your failure.

Nothing guarantees that a child will choose well, Charlie included. Thankfully, in his Spanish failure, Charlie got it and cared. He made the needed turnaround and accomplished a midcourse correction. The experience of near failure taught Charlie a valuable lifelong lesson, and he had many successes in future years. Failure in his Spanish lessons became a springboard to success in lessons about life.

# PART FOUR

# Reflecting on the Journey

During Tommy's childhood, you wonder
about his outcome—and you fret.
Difficulties with Tomi tempt you to fear what she thinks of you.
And you ask...
What will happen to this child?
Can good come out of this?
Will my active child ever change?
Will she consider all my efforts worth it someday?
Reflections on my journey deliver hope into your world called *hyper*.

# Thirty

## FLYING HIGH

The Boeing jumbo jet lumbered down O'Hare's runway, slowly rising into the sky with our family buckled in for the ride of our lives. We were moving to the Philippines with four children, ages nearly two to eight. After Mike's six-week trip, we'd packed our household, stuffed our suitcases, and said our goodbyes. Now with toys and books stashed into every carry-on, we settled in for a lo-o-o-o-n-g trip.

It wasn't the first time we'd traveled with the children. There'd been our family vacations to Lake of the Ozarks (eight hours) and long car trips to grandparents (eleven hours). But this trip *way* exceeded anything we'd ever done:

A one-hour flight to Chicago (in a tiny commuter plane)
Three hours at O'Hare
Ten hours over the Pacific Ocean
Overnight in an Alaskan hotel (unplanned emergency stop thanks to bad weather)

Two hours on the Anchorage tarmac (somebody forgot to load enough food for the galley kitchen)
Ten more hours over the Pacific
Seven hours of layover in the Tokyo airport (managing four sleepless children)
Four-hour flight to Manila
Two hours in customs (lugging eleven boxes, plus carry-ons, and, oh yes, kids)
Plus one hour in a van driving to the hotel. Equaled?
The travels equaled forty-eight hours!

Whew! Wow! We had accomplished a forty-eight-hour international trip with four young children.

In Manila as we debarked from the aircraft, a woman who had been on the flight since Chicago stopped us and said, "When I got on this plane and saw your family of four children, I groaned inside, dreading the noise and disorder of young kids. But I have to tell you how amazed I am. Your children have been incredibly well behaved, and you have my highest compliments."

It was true, and actually I was amazed, too. Our children *had* been incredibly cooperative for the entire trip, even six-year-old Charlie. As I listened to this woman praising our children, I thought, *Lady, you don't even know. You're talking about Charlie being well-behaved. Praise God!*

Though Charlie was still incredibly active, those forty-eight hours had revealed the headway he was making toward maturity. Had we turned a corner? Maybe? Time would tell.

Character development is a process. Do you keep longing, looking for some turning points in your Tommy? If visible turning points haven't come yet, resolve to stay on course with teaching him, and remain patient with his process of growing up. Each child arrives at forks in the road at different times in life, and you never know when those moments will come. Kids do grow up.

At the same time, we must face the reality that kids don't always "grow up," if you know what I mean. Maturity is unpredictable, and you can't have complete certainty about the outcome. People don't *automatically* mature into polite, well-behaved, civil individuals. We all know adults who seem about as mature as a four-year old throwing adult-sized tantrums. Our flight to Manila revealed Charlie's outward conformity, yet we couldn't know whether or not he had developed an inward desire for good. Any future change of heart was only for Charlie to know—and then to tell as his own story.

Over the years Charlie's outward maturity came in incremental steps, and as he got older, we began to notice changes in behavior. To be sure, he stayed as energetic as ever (in high school, his soccer team called him "Caffeine Bergen"), and he was still inclined to bug his siblings (habitually poking or grabbing them). But gradually Charlie began to notice other people's feelings, and he began to take responsibility for his impact. We can't begin to know all that contributed to this, but we do know we intentionally taught him two things.

First, during Charlie's early years, we taught him the standards of behavior that society expects. His energy level didn't deter us from imparting the standards: be kind, don't hit, do share, and so on. We taught him that his energy was good and could be used for good, but if he used it for harm, it could be incredibly destructive. We told him that his energy was like the power of water which could be channeled behind a dam for generating electricity; yet it could also be unleashed from a broken dam, destroying everything in sight. His energy was not bad. How he *used* his energy could be either good or bad—which would ultimately become his own choice. He began to internalize the standards.

As mentioned earlier, even though rewards and consequences are important for motivating outward self-control, child-raising "formulas" don't govern whether or not children will internalize the value of being good. That was true for Charlie and it's true for your children as well. Rules merely lay down the law to show children the standards and point the way (and love from you gives them a good example to imitate). Yet eventually they will have to make their own choices. "Will I become a person who truly cares for others?"

Over time I came to understand that I couldn't make Charlie, or any of my children, good on the *inside*. No parent on earth has the power or ability to do such a thing, and you don't either. I didn't understand this when I first had kids. Originally I had thought my role was to form my children into good citizens. I'd thought I could do this singlehandedly through following a good child-raising formula. Isn't that what a good parent is supposed to do? However, while helping Charlie learn to obey, eventually I came to see that my best efforts could only make him obedient on the outside but not in his heart.

My role as a parent was a lot like Moses in the Bible when he gave a nation the Ten Commandments. Like Moses, my role was to teach good and moral commands to my kids. But each of them possessed the actual decision of whether or not to obey. When they disobeyed, they reaped the consequences and learned that they had a problem. But when they saw their problem, more "law" from me didn't answer their problem. Moses' writings couldn't make the people good in their hearts.

Likewise, my rules/laws were just a tutor that would hopefully lead my children to the true source of goodness—their perfect, loving, and forgiving God. So my goal became to help the children see their *need* for inner goodness (hence, the rules) and point them to God's remarkable provision for them in Jesus Christ. My role of giving "rules to live by" was merely a step in the process, not the ultimate procurer of that process.

Because of this, our second intentional lesson for Charlie was truth about forgiveness. For anyone, and especially for the vivacious child, life brings mistakes and bad choices. Charlie was no exception. In his short lifetime, he had faced a bundle of negative consequences from his behavior. Biting your brother doesn't go unnoticed, neither does throwing rocks at people. And on and on... The standards had been broken, so we wanted Charlie to know that even though we gave consequences when his behavior didn't meet the standards, we still loved him no matter what. Even while enforcing consequences, my heart forgave him and I didn't hold misbehavior against him personally. I forgave. And God offered forgiveness, too.

In fact, Jesus had taken the rap for Charlie's, and everyone's, misdoings to such a degree that he'd paid the ultimate penalty—the death penalty—to become a substitute for every misdeed. How did we know it was the truth? I had reviewed compelling historical evidence from predictions about him before he ever lived (e.g., see Isaiah 53[27]), and I had studied evidence for his resurrection, conclusive evidence that established Jesus *had* come to life after dying.[28] This historical evidence had convinced me that two thousand years ago, a real person, Jesus Christ, had lived, died, been buried, and then had come out of his grave, *alive*. Because of the resurrection, I had the reason to believe that Jesus Christ was God, that he wanted to give everyone life after death, and that forgiveness from God was available for whoever believed and wanted to receive it. The Bible stated:

> *God had promised to raise him from the dead, not leaving him to rot in the grave... through this man Jesus there is forgiveness for your sins. Everyone who believes in him is made right in God's sight—something the law of Moses could never do.*
>
> (ACTS 13:34, 38)[29]

So what was Charlie's response? Well, remember, that's his own story to tell. But I do know that at about age five, he began to understand the concept of forgiveness. He knew we loved him, no matter what, and God did, too. And after that, I started noticing some turning points, like the flight to the Philippines.

# Thirty-one

## TO MATURITY AND BEYOND!

A robed procession flowed through the university auditorium, college graduates solemnly streaming to their seats. Looking over a sea of flat caps, I sat perched on a pinnacle of joy. As in a dream, I heard the Dean of Biological Sciences announce: "Charles Bergen."

But it wasn't a dream. Charlie walked across the stage, and my tears welled up as I watched this son shake the dean's hand and receive his bachelor's degree. Memories squeezed my heart....

This was the inconsolable infant who'd kept me awake, giving me ample time to pray and plead for him.

This was my precious toddler with twinkly eyes who wreaked havoc in the household.

This was the second grade boy whose active body and distracted mind had kept him from learning to read.

This was the high school student who had persevered and discovered how to study assignments, organize notebooks, and memorize lessons.

And now he was here, *and he was graduating from college.* I had spent many years in exhaustion, yet I had helped him come to this point of maturity. Oh, the joy!

Super-active little Charlie had matured into a super nice young man who was stepping into a bright future. Because of his inquisitive mind and his passionate quest for truth, he hoped to pursue graduate studies in genetics, seeking to unravel mysteries encrypted in DNA. I knew he could do it. And maybe in years to come, he could even be the one to unravel the genetic secrets of his own wiring. Maybe he would be the one to discover the mystery of why our super-active baby arrived so incredibly *wired*!

My sentimental reflections receded with the graduates' recessional. The stream of robes left the auditorium and entered the reception hall. Our happy family followed, ready to give high fives and snap photos. My eyes roamed the sea of black… and finally I saw him, and he spotted me… and…

…Sweet, sweet hug!

Sentimental moments. Successes. Dreams that come true. Gratitude from your child. For me these moments came at random times—Lego contests, Boy Scout events, and the church talent show. And yes, Charlie did graduate, but the point isn't that Charlie got a college degree. Not all children do, and that's perfectly fine. The point is you can know, in the end, that your blood, sweat, and tears are not a waste of time. The effort of mommy-hood is totally worth it.

Yet even if you never see the fruit of your effort during your child's lifetime, God knows your efforts. "For God is not unjust so as to forget your work and the love which you have shown…."[30] What a hope! Our heavenly Father is excited and happy about the love that you pour into your child each and every day. Being a dedicated mom to an incredibly valuable child is a wonderful investment.

# Thirty-two

## FINAL THOUGHTS

D o you wonder if adult Charlie still shows signs of being wired? Did he grow up to be completely calm and "normal" (whatever that is)? Well, here's the answer…

Though Charlie eventually matured into a wonderful, law-abiding citizen (*yay!*), some things never changed. His wiring is internal and permanent. I embrace this reality and love him for who he's wired to be. For example:

Charlie learned to sleep. *Kind of.* To this day he's a light sleeper, and he needs white noise or sleep eludes him.

Charlie learned to keep his hands and feet to himself. *Kind of.* In college he confided to me that the temptation still surfaced. What?

Charlie learned to study. *Kind of.* He didn't do well at homework unless he was in a quiet room by himself away from distractions.

Charlie's energy level eventually subdued. *Kind of.* Now while playing with nephews in their sandbox, Charlie's monster trucks fly through the sand *way* more energetically than the other uncle's trucks. And today, in the midst of all his workload, Charlie pursues community service with fervor (though now he says, "Naptime? That sounds nice!").

Charlie learned to pay attention. *Kind of.* To this day his ears frequently are deaf to the people around him, and my perpetual question remains, "Did Charlie hear me?" He's in the world of his own busy mind. If you say something to him, be aware there's a strong chance he hasn't listened. (Somebody bring on the ice cream!)

Don't expect your super-active Tommy or Tomi to become someone they are *not.* Just be ready to give them love for their entire life, accepting them for who they are. Meanwhile…

Maintain courage—you can and will make it to the end,
one hour and one minute at a time.
Keep perspective—your child is precious, having great intrinsic value.
Hang onto hope—your efforts are completely worth it all.

# Thirty-three

## CHARLIE'S LETTER TO YOU

Dear Mommy of Tomi or Tommy,

You've just read my mom's story about life with a hyperactive child and how she coped. Well, my name is Charlie, and since these stories were about me, after reading these stories, you're probably wondering about my opinion of my childhood! The short answer is that for me, it was a time of wonder and discovery, and I'm now grateful for all the effort my mom put into raising me.

Perhaps you have a child that currently is wearing you out or has you feeling like an inadequate parent. Although he or she may not say it now, allow me to say the words that they are not able to express: Thank you! Thank you for all of your unrelenting effort, love, and patience.

I really appreciate that my mom understood and supported my need to be energetic. As my mom said, energy is like water behind a dam. Reservoir water is used constructively to generate electricity, but that same water becomes destructive if the dam breaks. With that concept in mind, she helped me learn to harness my energy toward building things up, not tearing them down. My mom provided ways to use my energy constructively through active play, such as marching to music inside the house or splashing in the backyard pool. My mom understood that I needed to have constructive outlets for my energy, just as long as the outlet did not involve a sibling falling to the ground.

The impulse to trip my siblings was obviously a destructive aspect of my hyperactivity. Mom tried to teach me, but my impulsiveness was deeply ingrained. Even when I was in college, I remember sitting in the hallway eating lunch with my sister (because cafeteria seating was maxed out) while students walked by between classes. I asked Joy if she had the same problem that I had, where I had to keep telling myself not to stick out my leg to trip one of the unsuspecting students. Although this demonstrates that I had indeed mastered the art of directing my energy, it also shows that some elements of hyperactive wiring die hard.

One of the frustrations you may have is that your child does not pay attention, listen, or focus. You have read about my lack of focus. I would look at my mother's eyes but not listen to what she said, much to her dismay. Yet from my perspective (and my mom would agree now), I would say that I actually focused really well! It's just that my focus was not on the same things my parents wanted me to focus on. Instead of listening to my mom's instructions for chores, I would be thinking about how to build Legos. However, this same focus, when directed toward things in my older years, such as grad school and work, has been a huge strength. So just remember that the aspects of your child that seem like hardships may turn out to be a gift in the long run.

Another aspect from my perspective was that, as a child, life seemed normal. Although my mom felt many days were utter chaos, from my vantage point, everything was fine and life was great. Just like my mom mentioned, when we threw a special "King Party" for dad, what seemed like a disaster to her was a highlight of the year for me. Put in broader terms, what may seem like exhausting and draining years with a toddler or preschooler will likely seem like years of wonder, love, and excitement through your child's eyes.

Another thing that I want to tell you, and that I'm sure you are desperately wanting to hear, is that it is worth it. My mom's patience and love now mean the world to me. There's no one else that I would want as my mother, and I am forever grateful for her years of loving and raising me. She continues to be one of the people that I admire most, and I always know that she loves me with all her heart.

So I will say once more to all the moms of active children who are giving your child so much, "Thank you!"

Wishing you the best,
Charlie

# Bonus Section:
# FAQs and Tips for
# Family and Friends

# Faqs and Tips for
# Family and Friends

When Charlie was a one-year old, my husband and I desired to celebrate Christmas with our parents. So we strapped our boys into car seats, Charlie sporting ultra-cute toddler sunglasses, and drove 600 miles home. The sunglasses? Our solution to Charlie's hypersensitive trait of "too bright" during car rides.

Have you ever traveled with a hyper one-year old? It's no small feat! Munchies entertained, music tapes distracted (for a few minutes), and toys intermittently captured attention. We were grateful for Charlie's occasional naps.

Though I knew seeing our parents would be worth it in the end, the trip was grueling. Long after sundown we climbed the steps to my childhood home. My dad answered the door with open arms. As we all hugged, a most wonderful sight greeted me. I saw that my parents had constructed a barricade around the Christmas tree, a barricade made of coffee tables and overstuffed chairs. Our toddler-tornado would not be able to destroy the Christmas decorations this year—nor destroy our Christmas spirit. I was extremely grateful. They'd believed me, and they'd prepared!

My parents came through for us that Christmas, and I was incredibly thankful. My stories have also told you of others—Debbie, Marla, Karen, Libby, Lori, and other friends—who helped me over my bumps in the road. They didn't create ongoing dependency, but their availability in a time of crisis was invaluable. Anything that anyone did to lessen my load blessed me. Just to know they understood (to some degree) and desired to help was a great encouragement.

Every mother is surrounded by a balcony of people who both watch her and share her life. When a mom has an extra-active child, friends and relatives watch, and they can wonder, "What's going on with this craziness? Is there something I can do to help?"

The answer, of course, is, "Yes, it's crazy, and yes, you can help!"

At the same time, it's important to know there are also things that might not be all that helpful—and might even backfire. It's good to be informed about what is helpful and what is hurtful. The following are some frequently asked questions about hyperactivity, its effect in the home, and how to help an exhausted mom without it backfiring into harm. Take a minute to read these helps, and then go for it. You can make a difference in the life of your loved one, the one we've named Mommy of Tommy or Tomi.

By the way, if you are the Mommy of a Tommy who is reading this section, please interpret these tips as your permission to ask for help when you've hit that bump. Don't try to go it alone when in reality you are crashing. Do make requests. But when you do, try to ask for help without expectations. Most people really do want to know how they might help you, but they don't enjoy experiencing your anger if they're unavailable to help right now, so don't be demanding. But do let others know when you have a specific need.

## How can you know whether or not a child is hyperactive? *All children are active, aren't they?*

Yes, it's a *given* that moms everywhere are dealing with active children.

As stated by Mayo Clinic, "Most healthy children are inattentive, hyperactive or impulsive at one time or another. It's normal for pre-schoolers to have short attention spans and be unable to stick with one activity for long. Even in older children and teenagers, attention span often depends on the level of interest. The same is true of hyperactivity. Young children are naturally energetic—they often are still full of energy long after they've worn their parents out. In addition, some children just naturally have a higher activity level than others do."[31]

All children are active and some are extra-active. Whether your friend's child has a diagnosis of hyperactivity or not, if the activity level of the child has left the mom exhausted, that Mommy of Tomi needs your support. Because you are her friend, sister, mother, or spouse, *you* are in a unique position to encourage! If you know a mom who is tired or disheartened from nonstop busyness, the information in this book is for you.

## The child of my friend is extremely hyperactive. What causes this?

Much research has been done on attention deficit hyperactivity disorder (ADHD), and the research continues. Factors that may be involved include genetics (inherited traits), environment (including chemical exposure such as lead), and neurological problems at key moments of brain development. However, at this point no exact cause of ADHD has been determined.[32]

## Why is this child so out of control? Wouldn't a good dose of discipline calm this child?

Every child needs appropriate consequences for the choices they make. Time-outs and other consequences are an important part of teaching children to make wise choices. Hyperactive children, and all children, need to learn the realities of cause and effect in life. They need to learn that you reap what you sow, even when you are hyperactive.

However, discipline cannot change the starting point of a child's wiring; a hyperactive child's muscles will still be wired to move. Therefore, a hyperactive child often makes foolish choices at a hyperactive rate. This frequency of misbehavior gives the impression that he or she is more out of control than other children. However, a heightened activity level simply showcases normal childishness to a greater degree.

The mom is not the cause of hyperactivity, so it's important that you not blame the mom for the frequency of her child's foolishness. The hyperactive child has simply chosen to misbehave, as do all children. Try to have compassion on your friend because she has a nonstop job dealing with all the infractions (and they sometimes come at a frantic pace). Have mercy as she perseveres at applying appropriate consequences.

Remember, hyperactive children will not gain self-control in a day, and their wiring will be with them for life. Though the mom's consistent discipline can help the child, the mom cannot change a hyperactive bent.

## What can I do to encourage a Mommy of Tomi?

Here are some suggestions for encouraging your friend:

- First of all, listen to her. Listen to her stories. Understand her situation. Listen to her without the intention of giving advice. Often just listening to her *is* the encouragement she needs. Give an ear, without expecting to change anything.
- Ask her how you can support her. Your interest in helping will itself be an encouragement. Also, the question of "How can I help you?" acknowledges you value her uniqueness and need her input. You understand that what's helpful will be different for each person. (See below for some practical ideas.)
- When you hear all the problems a mom is having with her child, it's tempting to give advice on child management. But this probably won't encourage her. Advice on child-raising implies that if only she would do something different, she wouldn't have this problem. She may interpret advice as you saying it's her fault—that she's to blame. This is not encouraging to her.
- Use the stories in this book as examples for how to encourage a mom. For example, Chapter 2 encourages moms to celebrate their child's positive traits and hidden talents. But when a mom is overwhelmed by the child's negative behavior, she often has a hard time finding positive traits. Enter you. Look for the positives in the child, and speak good words to her about her Tomi. Refrain from negatively comparing her with other children because the mom is already fighting this

temptation herself. Likewise, every chapter of *Tommy's Wired* can help you discern how to encourage a mom.

## I have advice that I know would help. Can't I give *some* advice?

If the Mommy of Tomi or Tommy is asking you, "What should I do?" and you have something in mind that might help, offer it simply as an idea for her to consider. You can present it as "take it or leave it." Assure her that you're not offended if she decides not to use your advice. Simply leave it on the table for her to consider. Don't come across as a know-it-all or as a controller. Always remember, it's her life, not yours, and her decisions about child-raising are her own. And if she's not wanting advice, don't give it.

## I want to give some physical and emotional support. What is helpful? What isn't?

Here are some ways to provide relief for exhausted moms and some pitfalls to avoid:

- Again, first of all, listen. Ask her what kind of help she needs and listen carefully to her response. She will be the best resource for how to help her. When she gives ideas, respect her answer. Don't take over her life.
- Give her some specific offers of ways you're able and willing to help. Be sensitive to discern whether or not she wants the type of help you are offering. Some specific ideas follow.
- Offer to do some cleaning (e.g., clean a bathroom, wash dishes, vacuum carpets). Instead of telling her, "Let me know

if you need help," you might say, "I'm free on Tuesday, and I can come vacuum your carpets or do other cleaning if that would be a help to you."

- Offer to do her laundry or fold clean clothes.
- Drop off a meal.
- Pick up some groceries for her.
- Watch the children while she takes a nap.
- Offer to babysit while she gets some time away.
- Short is okay and often preferred. When providing help at her house, don't come with the expectation that you'll get to visit and talk for a while. If she obviously wants to talk, you can definitely engage her in conversation because that may be her biggest need of the moment. Yet there may be times when she needs your help but doesn't have time for a long chat. So don't come expecting a lengthy conversation as a given. For example, just drop off a meal, say "I love you," and leave.

An exhausted parent in crisis is often desperate for support. Your help can provide the boost that's needed to get a mom back on her feet.

While you're helping, remember that you won't be able to make the needs go away because there will be daily needs for months or years to come. Every bit of help will make a temporary difference, but it can't become the "final solution."

Even though your help in a crisis will be appreciated, most moms want to get back on their own feet for the ongoing care of their family. Support her plans for being on her own. When your help isn't needed any longer, don't take it personally. Be happy that she's able to be independent.

## My friend is extremely sad all the time. What should I do?

First of all, understand that the mom of a super-active child has lost the life she once knew—a life that was predictable and controllable. She is probably feeling, "I want my life back!" Any kind of loss leads to grief. Mommy-hood grief can come from loss of control, loss of sleep, loss of former identity, and many other things. Because of this, books or websites on grief are helpful resources. They will give ideas on how to relate to a person who is grieving losses. Discover what to say (and not say) and what to do (and not do) for a grieving person. Then you'll be able to relate to your friend in more helpful ways.

Most mothers can become temporarily overwhelmed by the exhaustion of nonstop work, sleep deprivation, and loss of control. However, occasionally the stress of motherhood leads to clinical depression. Don't *assume* depression, but if her sadness has lasted for several months, consider the possibility that she may need help beyond what you are able to give. A medical doctor and/or professional counselor may be able to help her in ways that you can't. Also, consider the possibility of helping financially if professional help is beyond her reach.

## Why does my loved one push me away when I try to help her?

There could be multiple reasons, but here are some common ones:

- Are you listening well? Everyone wants to be understood, moms included. If you are talking about yourself more than you are listening, she may pull away.
- Do you avoid giving advice? Hearing continual, unsolicited advice often causes a mom to stay at a distance. When she

tells you her problems, be sure you aren't trying to fix her or to change her child.

- Do you have expectations? When you give support, if you expect to accomplish things in a certain way (your way), she will eventually get frustrated and conclude, "Why bother."
- Are you making her acceptance of your help a part of your own emotional fix? All of us want to be loved and accepted, and you do, too. Unfortunately, we sometimes tie our need for acceptance to the tasks we do. So if you offer to help a mom and she turns you down, don't conclude "She doesn't love me." She probably loves you but doesn't need the particular thing that you offered. If you become offended, it's likely she will withdraw from you.
- When you help her, are you careful to do things her way? If a mom has to redo everything after you leave, it's no help at all. This gets discouraging and may result in her pulling back from you.
- Do you give space by respecting the amount of time that she welcomes your help and then leaving promptly? Mothers are rightly responsible for controlling time and space in their own home. If you don't respect her boundaries, she'll need to keep a distance from you in order to maintain control of her life. She is responsible for managing her life, and pulling away is a means for avoiding invasion of privacy.

By doing these things, you'll build trust. And when the Mommy of Tommy trusts you, and has no cause to keep a distance, she'll want you near.

## Any last words?

A kangaroo mommy stood behind me at the grocery checkout, jostling the infant in her carrier pouch. Or maybe she was a rabbit mommy since her cart overflowed with other children—one in the seat, one in the basket, and a fourth child on the prowl. Loading my grapes onto the conveyor belt, I heard her chide that prowling boy.

"Come back from the candy!"

For me this scene was *deja vu.*

"I had four children," I commented, hoping she wasn't offended by my intrusion into her bubble.

"In six years," I supplied. "And one was hyperactive."

Her eyes met mine. "My oldest is seven," she said, adding, "I know which one is my hyperactive one."

Of course.

Then with hungry eyes, she ventured, "It looks like you survived."

"Yes, I survived," I assured her. "And you will too. An hour, a minute at a time."

She sighed. "Sometimes I'm not so sure."

Sometimes a Mommy of a Tommy is not so sure she can survive. She knows which one is her active one, and there will be times she is filled with self-doubt and hopelessness—which means your affirmation is extremely important in this mom's life. As a friend or family member, you have a fantastic opportunity to encourage and help her. Use your opportunities wisely, and you'll provide some much-needed assistance and relief. You can make a difference.

Love this special woman above all odds—no matter the outcome of the child. Remember, Tommy is wired and mommy is tired. So stand by her and give empathy, even when there's nothing more you can do. Simply love.

# PHOTO GALLERY:
# SNAPSHOTS—INFANT TO TEEN

Charlie's arm waved like a flag in a hurricane.

John's train cake.
(Karen holding Charlie and me holding John)

An enthusiastic, smiling bundle of energy.

A motherhood journey with my sister.

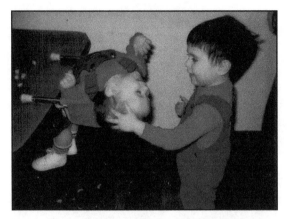

The high chair that Charlie couldn't escape.

Climbing up in microseconds (and he couldn't walk yet).

The Christmas barricade for our toddler-tornado.

Messy toddler.
(But at eighteen months he finally stayed in the high chair.)

Time for family fun—
a pretend campout in the backyard.

An energy outlet—splashing in the backyard pool.

Vaulting into the crib at age two.

And the twinkle never left.

Serenading baby Joy.

Acrobatics in the crab apple tree.

This Lego set included the shell of a motorboat.

Romping in the snow.

185

Joy, Grace, Charlie, and John.

In the "big picture"—children, cousins, and friends.

First place in the Lego contest.

Enjoying Metro Manila.

Active sons.

Caught on camera—an impulsive hug and a brother's elbow of self-defense while parents implore (behind clenched smiles), "Charlie! Don't bother John!"

I yelled, "Go Charlie!" from the sideline—and ruined the play.

Listening to a story while perched on the sofa.

International students in our "big picture" (with Charlie on top).

High school prom night.

And the energy goes on.

# Notes

## Introduction

[1] Goodwin, Shawn, medically reviewed by Timothy J. Legg, PhD, CRNP (February 24, 2016). "What Causes Hyperactivity?" *Healthline Newsletter.* https://www.healthline.com/symptom/hyperactivity.

## Chapter 4

[2] 2 Peter 3:7–10 NASB.

## Chapter 6

[3] Carpenter, Deborah (August 6, 2019). https://www.additudemag.com/behavior-punishment-parenting-child-with-adhd/

[4] Behavior and Disciple (menu). https://www.additudemag.com/category/parenting-adhd-kids/behavior-discipline/

[5] Positive Parenting (menu). https://www.additudemag.com/category/parenting-adhd-kids/positive-parenting/

## Chapter 7

[6] Trautner, T. (September 20, 2018). Overprotective parenting style. http://www.canr.msu.edu/news/overprotective_parenting_style.

[7] Lents, N. H., PhD (August 28, 2016). Yes, Overprotective Parenting Harms Kids. https://www.psychologytoday.com/us/blog/beastly-behavior/201608/yes-overprotective-parenting-harms-kids.

## Chapter 10

[8] 2 Corinthians 13:7 NASB.

## Chapter 14

[9] Psalm 75:3 NLT.

[10] Psalm 46:1 NASB.

## Chapter 15

[11] Brady, Carol, PhD (August 6, 2019). https://www.additudemag.com/stop-hitting/

## Chapter 17

[12]   Hebrews 12:2 NASB.

[13]   John 3:16 NASB.

[14]   Romans 5:1–11 NASB.

[15]   Ephesians (all) NASB.

[16]   1 Corinthians 1:30 NASB.

## Chapter 18

[17]   Harvard Health Publishing. "In Praise of Gratitude - Harvard Health." *Harvard Health Blog.* https://www.health.harvard.edu/newsletter_article/in-praise-of-gratitude.

[18]   "7 Scientifically Proven Benefits of Gratitude." *Psychology Today,* Sussex Publishers, from https://www.psychologytoday.com/us/blog/what-mentally-strong-people-dont-do/201504/7-scientifically-proven-benefits-gratitude.

## Chapter 20

[19]   Graham, Ruth Bell. *It's My Turn.* Flemming H Revell, 1982.

[20]   Psalm 27:13–14 NASB.

## Chapter 21

[21]   Young, Pam. *Sidetracked Home Executives.* Warner Books, revised and updated edition, 2001.

[22]   Ibid, p. 27.

## Chapter 25

[23]   Vanderhorst, Kim, personal communication. April 11, 2018.

## Chapter 26

[24]   Tobias, Cynthia. Resources (menu). https://cynthiatobias.com/resources-2/resources/

## Chapter 27

[25]   *Caring about Kids: Helping the Hyperactive Child,* National Institute of Mental Health, 1985. p 7.

## Chapter 28

26 Organizing Your Child (menu). https://www.additudemag.com/category/parenting-adhd-kids/organizing-your-child/

## Chapter 30

27 Isaiah 53 NASB.

28 McDowell, Josh and Sean McDowell, PhD. *Evidence That Demands a Verdict*. Harper Collins, 2017.

29 Acts 13:34, 38 NLT.

## Chapter 31

30 Hebrews 6:10 NASB.

## Bonus Section

31 Attention-deficit/hyperactivity disorder (ADHD) in children (August 16, 2017). *Mayo Clinic*. Mayo Foundation for Medical Education and Research. http://www.mayoclinic.org/diseases-conditions/adhd/symptoms-causes/dxc-20196181.

32 Ibid.

# Acknowledgments

To the cast and crew who lived this book, and to the balcony of people who supported it, thank you!

Thanks to the Heart of America Christian Writers Network. You all are the best. Thanks for affirming and encouraging every new writer. And thanks for the top-notch faculty you bring to conferences.

Thanks to the HACWN conference faculty who believed in this mission to mommies of Tommys: Sally, Les, B.J., Bob, Marrianne, and Catherine, your suggestions were golden. Thanks for being cheerleaders.

Thanks to the Elm Hill team. What an awesome crew. You took on the role of shepherd and staff, providing invaluable expertise for this project.

Thanks to Kelli, Kim, Sarah, EnLiang, Cam, Janel, Lori, and Dotty for reviewing the manuscript drafts and giving helpful suggestions. Thanks to those in that group who are licensed counselors, who took time to review content and vet it for clinical accuracy. And a special thanks to the mommy reviewers who have their hands full with caring for active children. By taking the time to read this book, you confirmed that any busy mom could do it.

Many thanks to my church friends, both pre- and post-Manila years: Debbie, Lori, Sharon, Libby, Cathi, Vicki, Mary Rose, Marna, Amy, Mardean, Donna, Rose, Angie, and Stella, I owe so much to you and to so many others. You, and all my unnamed friends, were everything during my stormy days—balcony, crew, and cast.

Lori, thanks for the validation and courage you gave in the midst of my cyclone when you said, "Rita, someday you'll write a book." Here it is!

Many thanks to my care, prayer, and share groups in the Kansas City metro. Your prayers and support have carried me through these months of writing, and words aren't enough to express my deep appreciation.

And thanks from the bottom of my heart to the cast of this story. I'm grateful for my mother and mother-in-law for their part in shaping me into the mother I became. A huge thanks to my sister, Marla, and sister-in-law, Karen, for propping me up through every season of life. You both have been the best friends I could ever want! Mega-thanks to John, Charlie, Joy, and Grace. This story wouldn't have been written without you, literally! And Grace, thanks so much for the expertise and impetus you gave toward publishing. You are the reason this book is in print.

Finally, Mike, you have been my greatest supporter in everything, and I appreciate you to the stars. I would nominate you for Best Actor only I know it hasn't been an act. Your heart of love for God shines, and I know you do it all for him, as you've said so many times, "All because of Jesus." I agree, which means this chance to share our hyperactive child story has been made possible all because of Jesus. So now we can say together, "Thank you, Lord."

# About the Author

Rita Bergen's various occupations include homemaker, teacher, author, and mentor of women. A graduate of the University of Kansas in elementary education and nutrition studies, Rita used her training to homeschool her children (elementary and middle school) and later to facilitate tutorial workshops for college students with neurological differences (including attention deficit hyperactivity disorder and autism spectrum disorder). Mother of four, grandmother of eight, and mentor to many, Rita now lives in the Kansas City metro area with her husband of thirty-nine years. She desires to encourage women in values-based living, inspiring courage for facing the challenges of life. You can contact Rita on her website at ritabergen.com or send a Facebook message through her page, Rita Bergen Author (facebook.com/ritabergenauthor/).

For additional resources, visit:
30secondsforhope.com

# 30 Seconds for Hope
Hope on the Fly for Moms on the Go

CPSIA information can be obtained
at www.ICGtesting.com
Printed in the USA
LVHW102145200320
650766LV00005B/9